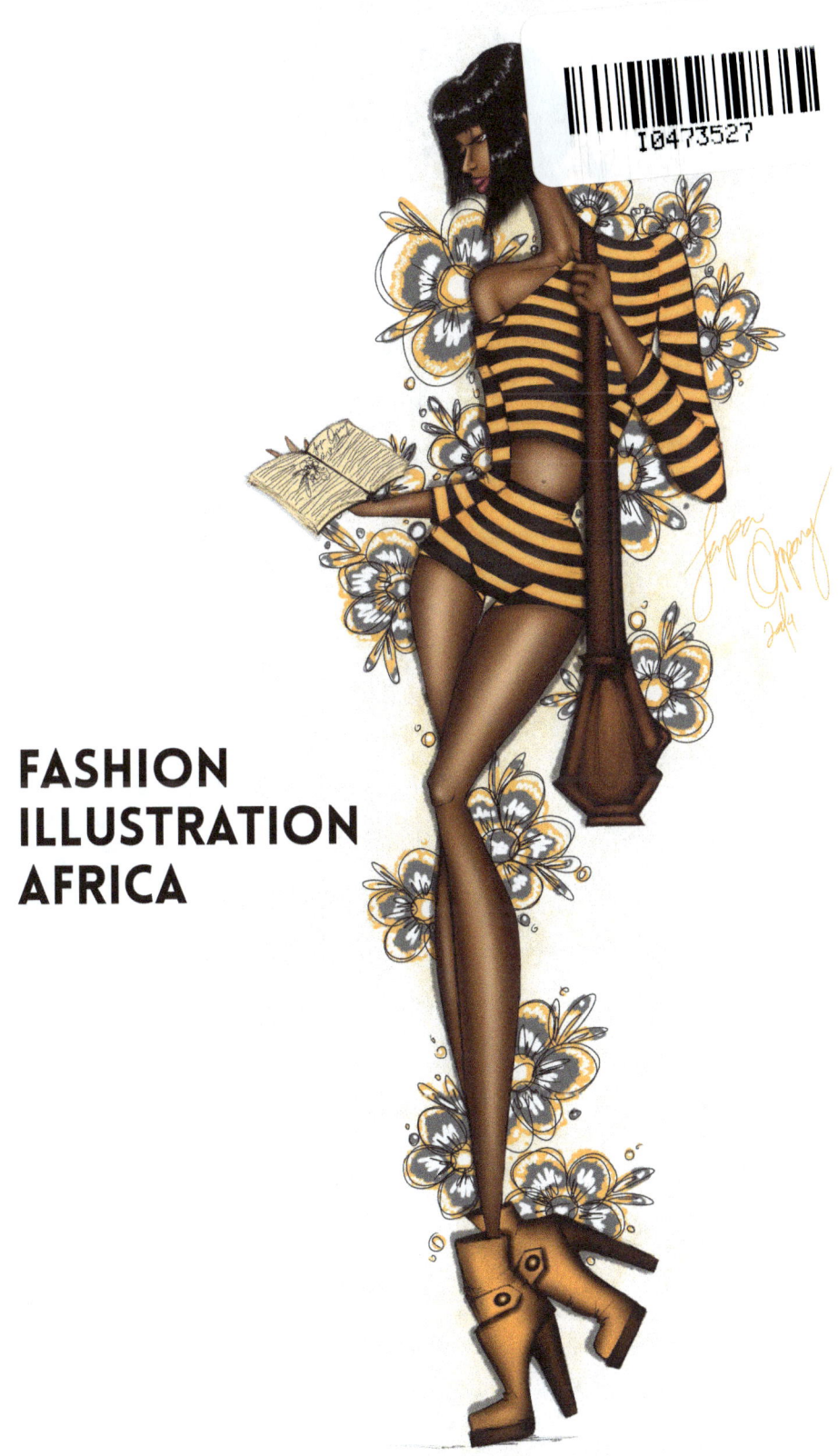

FASHION
ILLUSTRATION
AFRICA

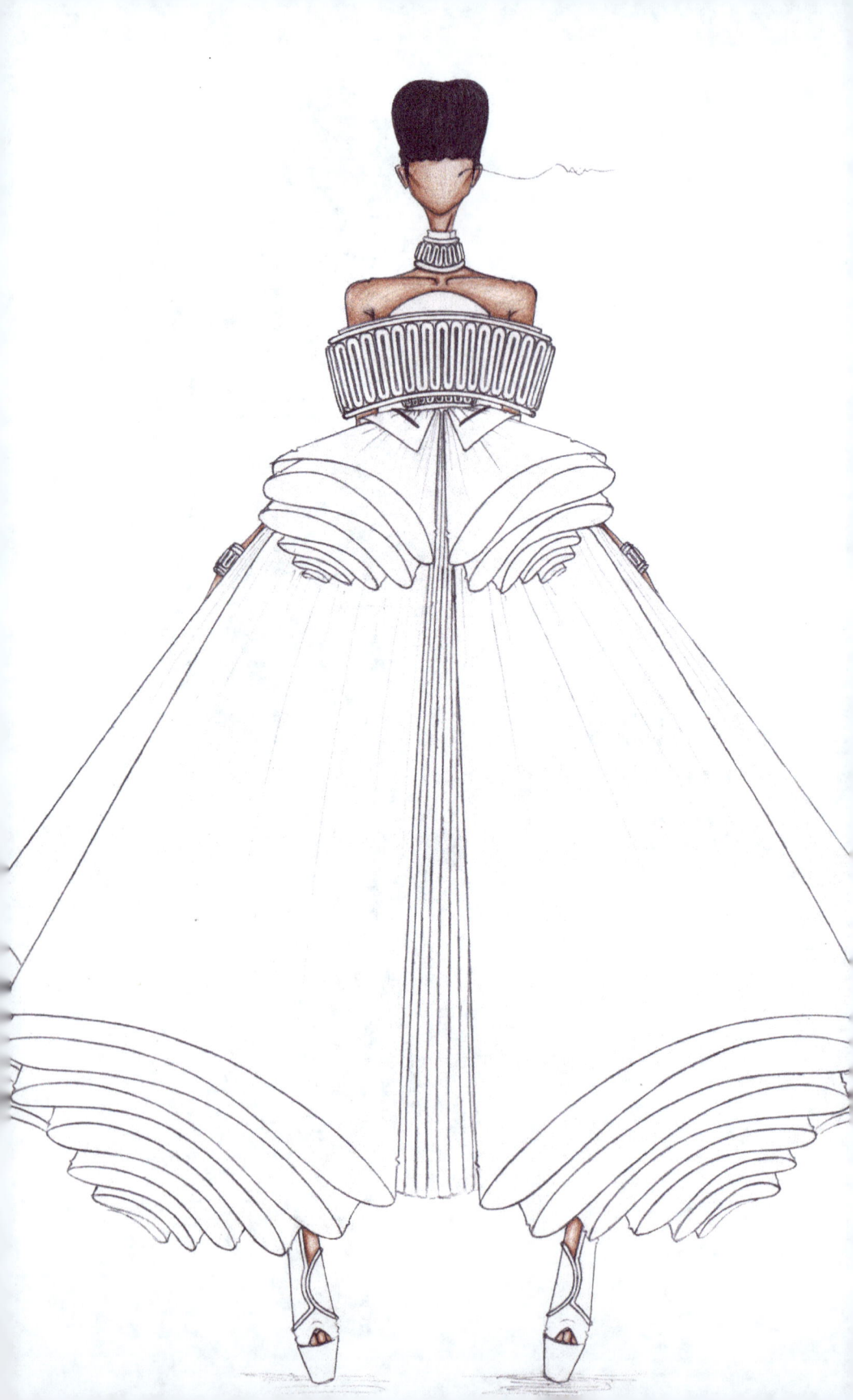

FASHION ILLUSTRATION AFRICA

A NEW GENERATION

Tapiwa Matsinde

Introduction by Zakirah Rabaney

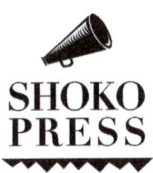

SHOKO
PRESS

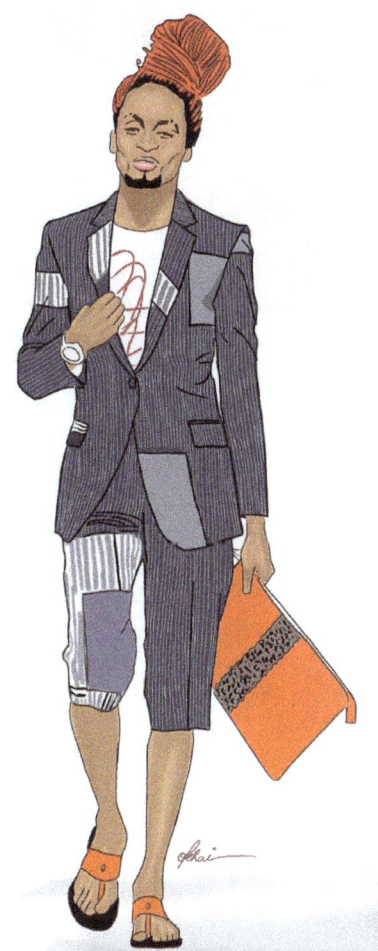

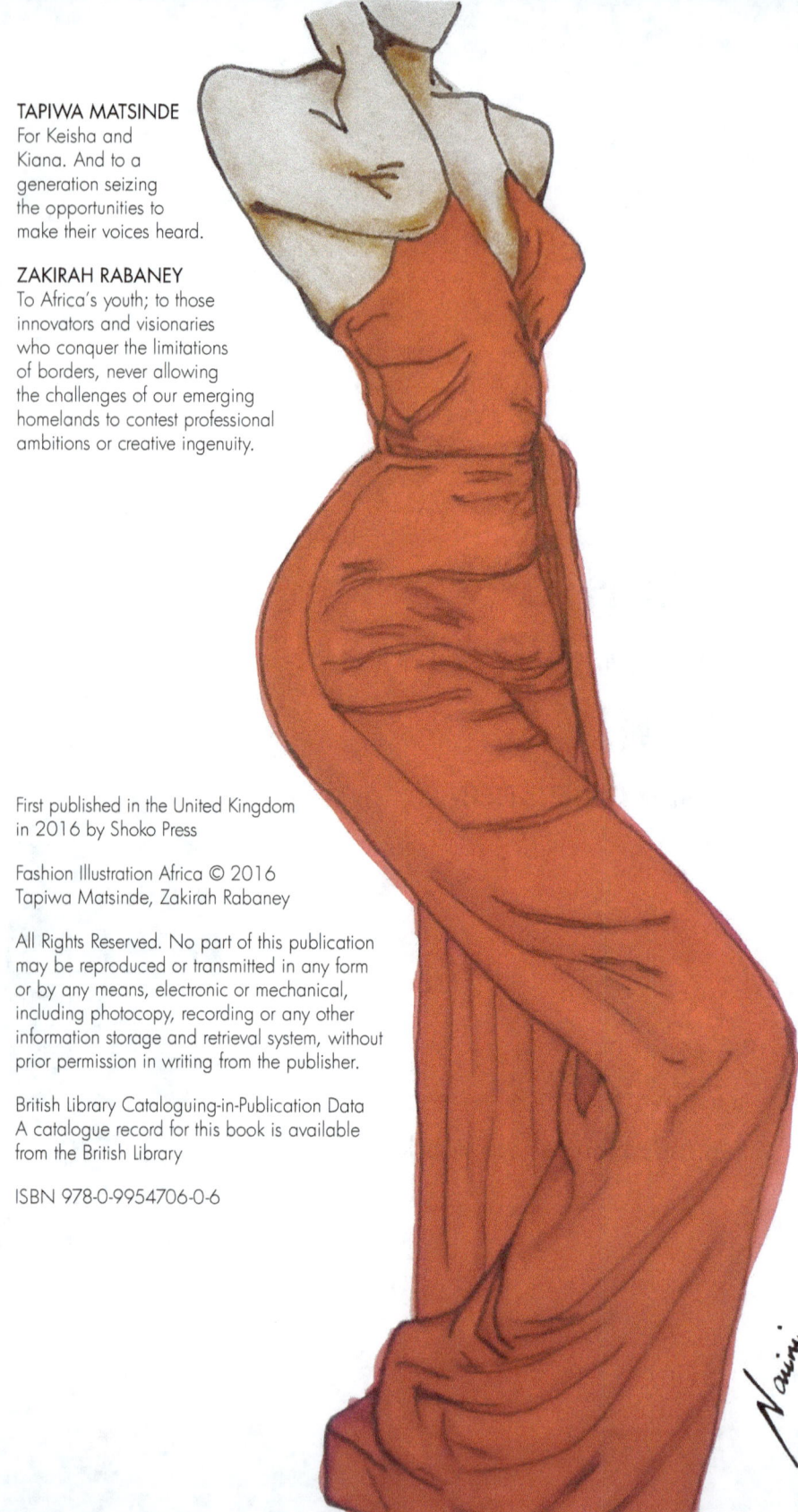

TAPIWA MATSINDE
For Keisha and
Kiana. And to a
generation seizing
the opportunities to
make their voices heard.

ZAKIRAH RABANEY
To Africa's youth; to those
innovators and visionaries
who conquer the limitations
of borders, never allowing
the challenges of our emerging
homelands to contest professional
ambitions or creative ingenuity.

First published in the United Kingdom
in 2016 by Shoko Press

Fashion Illustration Africa © 2016
Tapiwa Matsinde, Zakirah Rabaney

British Library Cataloguing-in-Publication Data
A catalogue record for this book is available
from the British Library

ISBN 978-0-9954706-0-6

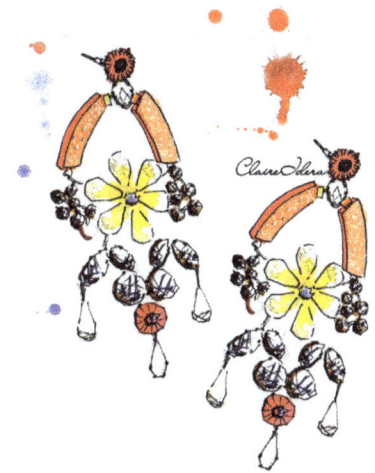

CONTENTS

Page 1: Papa Oppong, *The Reading Generation*, digital illustration, 2014
Page 2: Nathaniel Adjei Bio, *Glory Days, Look 3*, ink on paper, 2016
Page 3: Okhai, *Looks from Lagos Fashion Week*, digital illustration, 2015
Opposite: Nanini, *Shy*, pen and marker pen, 2016
This page: Claire Idera, *Ear Jewel*, mixed media, 2015

INTRODUCTION
BY ZAKIRAH RABANEY

The purpose of fashion illustration has greatly evolved since its origins over 500 years ago. Today, the drawing of clothing is about so much more than the representation of a design: it is about resuscitating an appreciation for originality in an age of mass production and reproduction; revelling in how artistic interpretations can reimagine the clothing we wear with sentiment and individuality; and balancing the advancement of fashion reportage and communication in our digital age.

Fashion illustration today also opens the door internationally to the perspectives of the African fashion illustrators featured in this book, allowing their work to be brushed by the distinctive aestheticism of their heritage while bordered by the western world and its global pop culture; revealing Africa as the artistic, fashion-conscious continent that it is.

As a proud South African fashion editor, stylist, trend analyst, writer and fashion illustrator working in a predominantly Western-orientated fashion industry, I see fashion illustration in Africa as a visual medium through which young African creatives are able to share their narratives about fashion, style and culture while still working within the context of an artistic discipline rooted in history. This history spans several centuries and tells a long tale of how the relentless advancement of technology truly was (and still is), fashion illustration's greatest antagonist – and how it became the African fashion illustrator's unlikeliest of heroes.

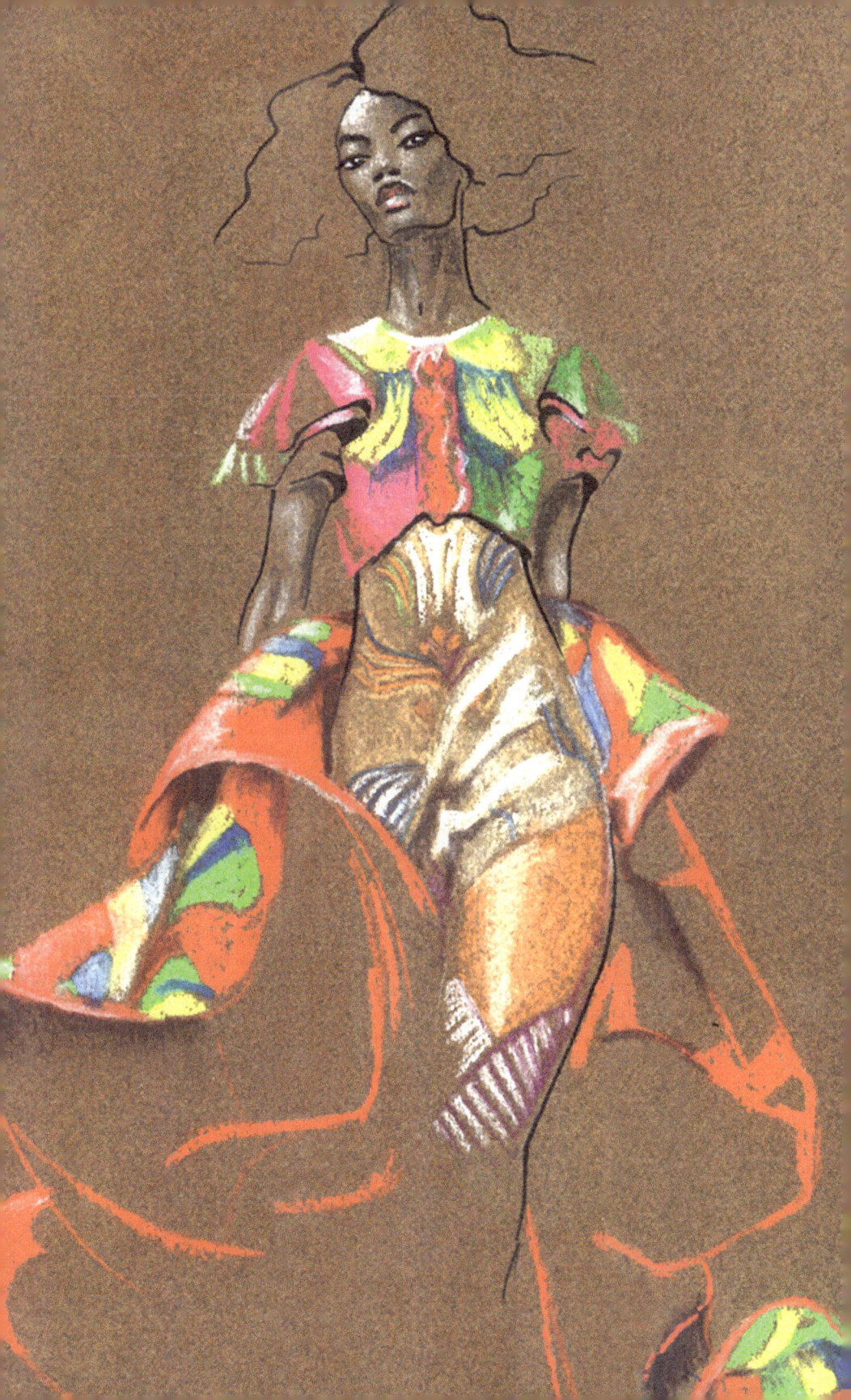

THE STORY OF FASHION ILLUSTRATION

From the coloured tomb paintings of the Ancient Egyptians in 3000 BC to the remarkable Buddhist art discovered on China's ancient Silk Road in the Mogao caves of Dunhuang, since humans could sculpt, paint, engrave and sketch, visual representations of clothing have existed. Although in these earlier times the depiction of clothing in art mostly chronicled ceremonial, historical or cultural events, fashion's universal ability to represent and communicate gender, status, tradition, social rank, occupation and culture, has always captivated us. It is these explanatory qualities about clothing that have motivated the development of the artistic discipline of fashion illustration.

During western Europe's *Age of Exploration* (beginning in the fifteenth century), seafaring explorers returned to Europe with reports of the discoveries of foreign lands, and European interest expanded to these newly-discovered peoples; how they looked, and ultimately, how they dressed. By the sixteenth century, this cultural curiosity initiated a visual accounting of the traditional costumes of these foreign populations in what was known as 'costume books', the first of which was published in Venice in 1558, and continued throughout the late sixteenth and early seventeenth centuries. The primary purpose of the earliest examples of fashion illustration in costume books was to accurately describe the fashion of populations from nations all over the world – including Africa and Asia. They were also used as an educational tool concerned with the accurate depiction and documentation of clothing.

By the seventeenth century, fashion illustration began its transition from these informative, sartorial diagrams, into an early form of fashion reportage. This new type of imagery, dedicated solely to fashion, endured. In France, picture books created by court engravers in the 1620s and 1630s portrayed how the nobility dressed. While in England, the famous etcher, Wenceslaus Hollar, created a detailed series of fashion illustrations in 1640 depicting the dress of women from all social classes. In 1672, during the reign of King Louis XIV of France, an official royal historian published a journal called *Le Mercure galant*, which issued the first forms of style reportage through text and fashion imagery. This journal, though not entirely dedicated to fashion, published a couple of fashion illustrations, as well as reports on the new seasonal trends and was divided into seasons like spring and fall. It also described the new styles of dress, textiles and trimmings worn by the French upper classes. Due to the successful influence of *Le Mercure galant* in Europe, as well as other articles and periodicals discussing style and exhibiting fashion imagery, by the end of the seventeenth century, fashion publications became an important channel for fashion illustrations. However, illustrations were still rare features in newspapers and other periodicals.

It was only during the second half of the eighteenth century, in places like England, France, Germany and Italy, that publishers began issuing regular columns, illustrations and sometimes even entire periodicals dedicated to fashion. During this time, fashion illustrations not only offered the average European or American woman living in the eighteenth century access to the wardrobes of the aristocracy, but also to visual narratives of who, how, when, why and where these dresses might have been worn. Furthermore, the rise of formal fashion magazines in the late eighteenth century took fashion illustration even further from its original purpose in costume books, transforming it into an agent for the dissemination of fashion and beauty values. Fashion illustration's ability to influence and interest its audiences during the nineteenth century can be measured by the hundreds of fashion periodicals that emerged in that period. As readerships grew, so did the need for these periodicals to be supplemented with fashion imagery. However, the invention of photography in the nineteenth century meant that a battle between fashion illustration and fashion photography soon followed.

At the turn of the twentieth century, fashion illustration was still enjoying prominent positions on the front covers of fashion magazines, and although photography was beginning to creep onto the fashion pages of *Vogue* and *Harper's Bazaar*, illustration and photography enjoyed equal status as fashion's ideal medium. During the first half of the twentieth century, new fashion magazines were still being printed and designers like Paul Poiret elevated fashion illustration in the hierarchy of fine art by commissioning artists to interpret his elaborate designs. If there were a golden age for fashion illustration, it would have been the 1920s and early 1930s. By 1932, however, *Vogue* had printed its first photographic cover, and by the 1950s, photography had become the dominant medium for fashion. Its immediacy, reproduction qualities and true-to-life recording abilities, made photography the most modern way to document and disseminate fashion. In the second half of the twentieth century, some fashion magazines did use fashion illustration as a creative way to portray trends, a novel medium for fashion advertisements, or occasionally, a cheaper alternative to photography. However, despite a brief revival during the 1980s, it was clear that fashion illustration's unrivalled run as fashion's primary visual medium had drawn to a close, and it almost completely disappeared from the covers and pages of fashion magazines.

AN UNEXPECTED TURN

In today's digital age, where attention spans are short and pictures are the new words, fashion illustration has been experiencing a renaissance. This revival can be seen as an artistic response not only to the ubiquity of digital photography in the twenty-first century, but could also be understood as a nostalgic reaction to the homogeneity in visual fashion reportage today, where the fashion press uses similarly shot runway photographs to report on similar trends every season. Fashion editorials also struggle to stand out, especially when editors only show certain looks depending on what the trends are. Nothing captures the imagination quite like the originality, sentiment and craft of a hand-drawn fashion illustration – the ideal balance to modern fashion communication's overemployment of photography and homogeneous visual content. Although pen and paint can never record detail as a camera does, fashion illustration does allow reality to be re-imagined through the illustrator's creative ingenuity.

Digital technology has abetted African fashion illustrators to work within the inner circles of the global fashion industry – an industry that is still dominated by the United States and western Europe. The phenomenon of social media technology in the twenty-first century, as well as the Internet's border-crossing abilities, has allowed for an emerging young and digitally savvy generation of fashion illustrators to include themselves in the global fashion dialogue. Blogging platforms such as Tumblr and social media apps such as Instagram have served illustrators as creative outlets, portfolios, public relations agents and even exhibition spaces. During a television interview for CNN's *African Voices*, Ghanaian fashion designer and fashion illustrator, Papa Oppong (p70), revealed how through sharing his fashion illustrations on Instagram, the international pop-star, Rihanna, 'followed' him on the image sharing app, joining Oppong's 15,000+ Instagram followers. Nigerian fashion illustrator, Adesola Lasisi (p16), claims the discovery of American-based fashion illustrator, Holly Nichol's work on Instagram prompted her to research fashion illustration online. She was soon hooked, and has been illustrating ever since. LeeAnn Visser (p34) recalls how overwhelmed she became with the level of feedback and exposure she received when she started to post her work online. Similarly, after Nanini (p46) posted her first fashion illustration on Instagram, she describes how the positive responses inspired the realisation that a market for fashion illustration does in fact exist. So naturally, Nathaniel Adjei Bio (p48) advises aspiring fashion illustrators to, 'be best friends with social media because that's your only portal to reach the millions of people out there waiting to get a glimpse of your greatness.' Social media's capacity to connect and promote, and – crucially – amass a large number of followers in a relatively short period, is an experience shared by many of the fashion illustrators in Africa.

ILLUSTRATING THE AFRICAN NARRATIVE

Fashion illustration's present renaissance affects and includes Africa's fashion illustrators by shining a light on the continent's creative and fashion-conscious youth. Today young African fashion illustrators are using the medium as a conduit to express both contemporary and traditional African aesthetics, which are not only informed by global pop culture, but also contribute to the fashion illustration diaspora through the work they share on the Internet and social media. And what makes their content so compelling is their unique aesthetic that is very different to established styles of fashion illustration. Where the content of western fashion illustration often focuses on luxury fashion brands, trends and the latest runway collections, young African fashion illustrators are driven less by commerce and more by a grassroots love of fashion, which also reflects strong visual cultural identities. When explaining her personal style of illustration, Cameroonian-American illustrator, Nyorh Agwe (p62), connects her practice – which focuses on bold colours, patterns, line variations and a love for playing with scale – to her Cameroonian background. She explains, 'that is how Cameroonians dress: big, bold, colourful and dramatic. It comes naturally because I am more drawn to this type of aesthetic than anything.' Similarly, London's Central Saint Martins graduate, Michelle Njeri Cuthbert (p42), traces her earliest influences back to Sunday afternoons in Kenya, when her mother would encourage her to trace the political cartoons printed in the weekend newspaper.

There are an assortment of methods and mediums being used across the African continent to create fashion illustrations, but for most illustrators, the choice is usually rooted in how easy it is for them to control their elected medium. For example, watercolour paint and inks are notorious for their unruly qualities; whereas acrylic paint, marker pens, pencil crayons, pens, pastels and charcoal are much easier to handle and manipulate. Some fashion illustrators, for example Nelly Aba Mensah (p52), select their medium based on what they are trying to depict, as Mensah says, 'I usually think about the subject first: what materials is the dress made of; do I want to emphasize colour or just shapes and lines? Just as one outfit isn't made of the same fabric, but rather a combination of materials, sequins, buttons etc., my drawings are also made with different elements rendered in whatever medium can convey their nature best.'

Developments in digital technology have also had an impact on the mediums used in illustration. The debate about hand-drawn versus computer-generated images continues to be a highly polarized one. Nigerian fashion illustrator, UdegbunamTBJ (p92), believes hand-drawn fashion illustrations are good but also states: 'drawing digitally is way better because there's almost a 100% flexibility that comes with it.' Kyere Kwaku Awiti (p30) from Ghana agrees, stating that ever since he started creating fashion illustrations, he has been using computers because he finds wet media too difficult to control. Peniel Enchill (p74), started using acrylic paint as her primary medium, but she is now a firm believer in utilizing digital software to create her vivacious fashion illustrations. There is, however, a noticeable preference for combining hand-drawn and computer-generated mediums. Fine and applied arts graduate, Ibe Ananaba (p22), enjoys each medium he uses regardless of whether it is operated by hand or computer: 'Ballpoint pen is bliss when the ink flows smoothly ... With watercolour, I like the fact that it puts my confidence and decision-making to test. It's a dicey medium that could be so tough to control. It takes me on an enjoyable adventure … For acrylic, it's fun when I'm a bit impatient. The fast drying nature of it thrills me. Other mediums like charcoal, markers, oil paint and so on have their specific reasons I enjoy them. Digital mediums are interesting as well … The fact that one can 'undo' a command is an open door to countless things.'

Anime-inspired illustrator, Pola Maneli (p78), also likes to combine hand-drawn and digital techniques, saying: 'I love the feeling of pencil on paper, but the overwhelming majority of my work is digitally finished. So I usually do as many pencil studies/warm-ups as I can. Then I draw the compositions in pencil and render them digitally.' Finally, as a fashion illustrator myself, I can also corroborate the virtues of digitally produced imagery, but tend to lean more towards hand-drawn fashion illustrations. My work (p100) is littered with unintended paint splatters and not-so-steady brushstrokes, but I see those as fundamental features attesting to the techniques I have used and their authenticity. Ultimately, it is a matter of personal preference, as different mediums and methods each harness different results.

The way that illustrators stylize the characters they depict is also an important aspect of the genre in Africa – fashion illustration is not always only about the clothing, but the personalities of the figures they dress too. Self-taught artist and graphic designer, Tonderai's (p90), colourful and realistic work is unlike the idealized figures one usually associates with fashion illustration. Yega (p96) favours realistic depictions of women in fashion and describes her work as traditional because it is true-to-form and lifelike.

MEETING CHALLENGES WITH FRESH VIEWPOINTS

There are also many challenges and stereotypes about fashion illustration that these illustrators hope to break. Ese Akpojotor, founder and designer of Sweet Design Studio (p86), describes her experience: 'I find it very very elitist. You have to illustrate white women in couture clothing to even be considered a fashion illustrator, which I think is so wrong because fashion is universal and diverse and should be represented realistically.' South African fashion illustrator, Lindsay Dhludhlu (p38), puts it: 'I live in the southern part of Africa, and as a [developing] country the discipline of fashion illustration is perceived as three main themes. The first is primitive or historic – people think [that in order] to relate to Africans illustrations should consist of animal skin, the texture of ethnic hair and serene landscape views. The second is to oversexualize women whilst conveying a sense of activity taking place: women playing sport, women as maids cleaning or women in the office holding a position of authority. The third is to feed into the idea of being modern or "futuristic" but really taking what has already been done in [developed] countries and try to incorporate it into our own.'

Dhuldhlu also believes that fashion illustrators have a significant role to play in their local fashion industries. She highlights the thriving talent pool in her own country but acknowledges that the lack of knowledge, resources and infrastructure can be crippling, explaining, 'The opportunities are there but because of the costs, fashion designers, stylists, editors and media such as magazines and books will not want to work with [South African] fashion illustrators unless they are multi-disciplined or versatile with the line of work they do.' Algerian fashion illustrator,

Sonia Merabet (p82), mirrors Dhludhlu's opinion and explains that in Algeria, the fashion industry is not developed enough to support fashion illustration as an art form, let alone as a career warranting paid incentive. Ghanaian fashion illustrator, Kobby Adu (p26), however, feels there is an ironic disconnection between the appreciation for art and the appreciation of artists by African people: 'It's actually quite strange. In my one and a half years of being back in Ghana, I have actually noticed that, on a continent where art is so ubiquitous and such an indelible part of our separate cultures, we tend not to respect occupations in it as much as others.'

There are many things that need to change to support the future of fashion illustration in Africa, but some of Africa's fashion illustrators are taking it upon themselves to be the catalysts for this change. For example, in order to bring more awareness to the discipline, Claire Idera (p18), has started training others in the art of fashion illustration, having observed the growing number of people who are interested. Okhai, aka Lean Kid (p66), also explained that fashion illustration is becoming more recognized as a way for designers and stylists to bring their designs and look books to life.

The young fashion illustrators featured in this book are far from naïve about the challenges that face them, and choose to illustrate their own way forward. Their global dialogue and emphasis on the preservation of their heritage in their artwork is a significant testimony of this generation's self-awareness; a self-awareness that is important for the future development of the African continent, and is certainly not just for the sake of it. Articulated in the words of successful fashion artist and illustrator, Nicole Cronje (p56), 'As Africans we have a unique perspective on life, one that is still in the early stages of being expressed. We are exposed to the soul of a land that is abundant in beauty and creative spirit. It is our privilege as artists to translate the language of this into something the world can follow. I believe the fashion industry in particular, is thirsty for an African viewpoint.'

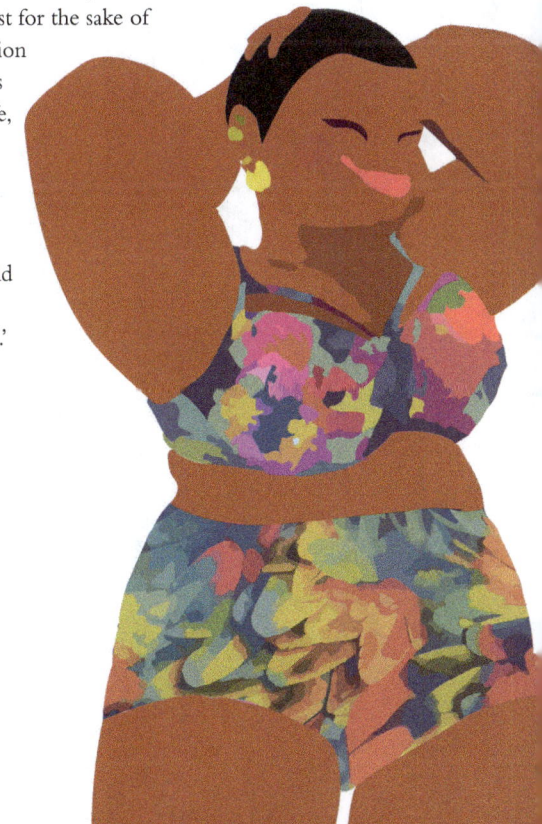

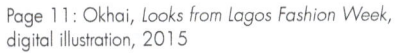
Page 11: Okhai, *Looks from Lagos Fashion Week*, digital illustration, 2015

This page: Lindsay Dhludhlu, *Untitled*, digital illustration, 2014

Overleaf: Papa Oppong, *A Celebration of Art*, digital illustration, 2015

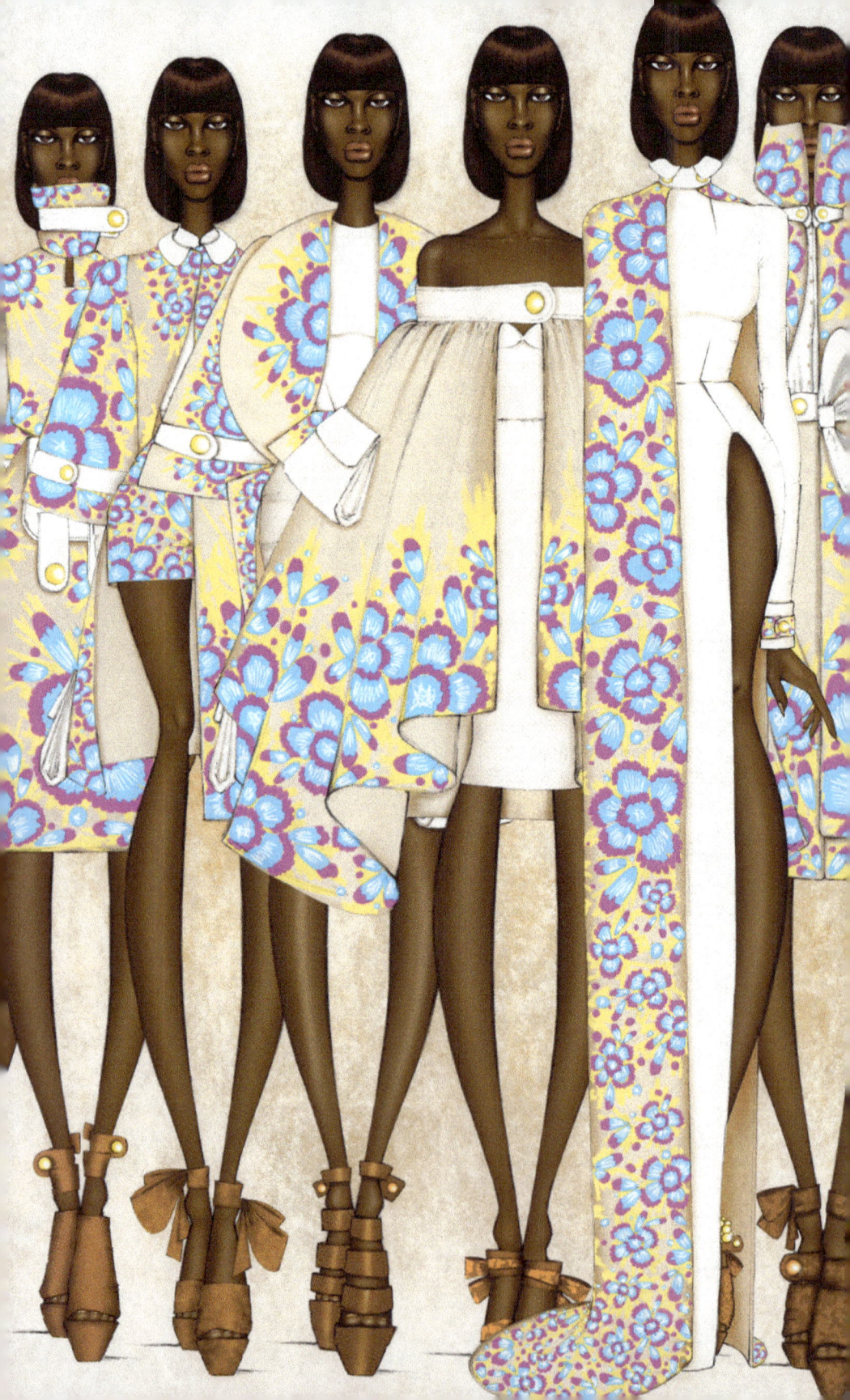

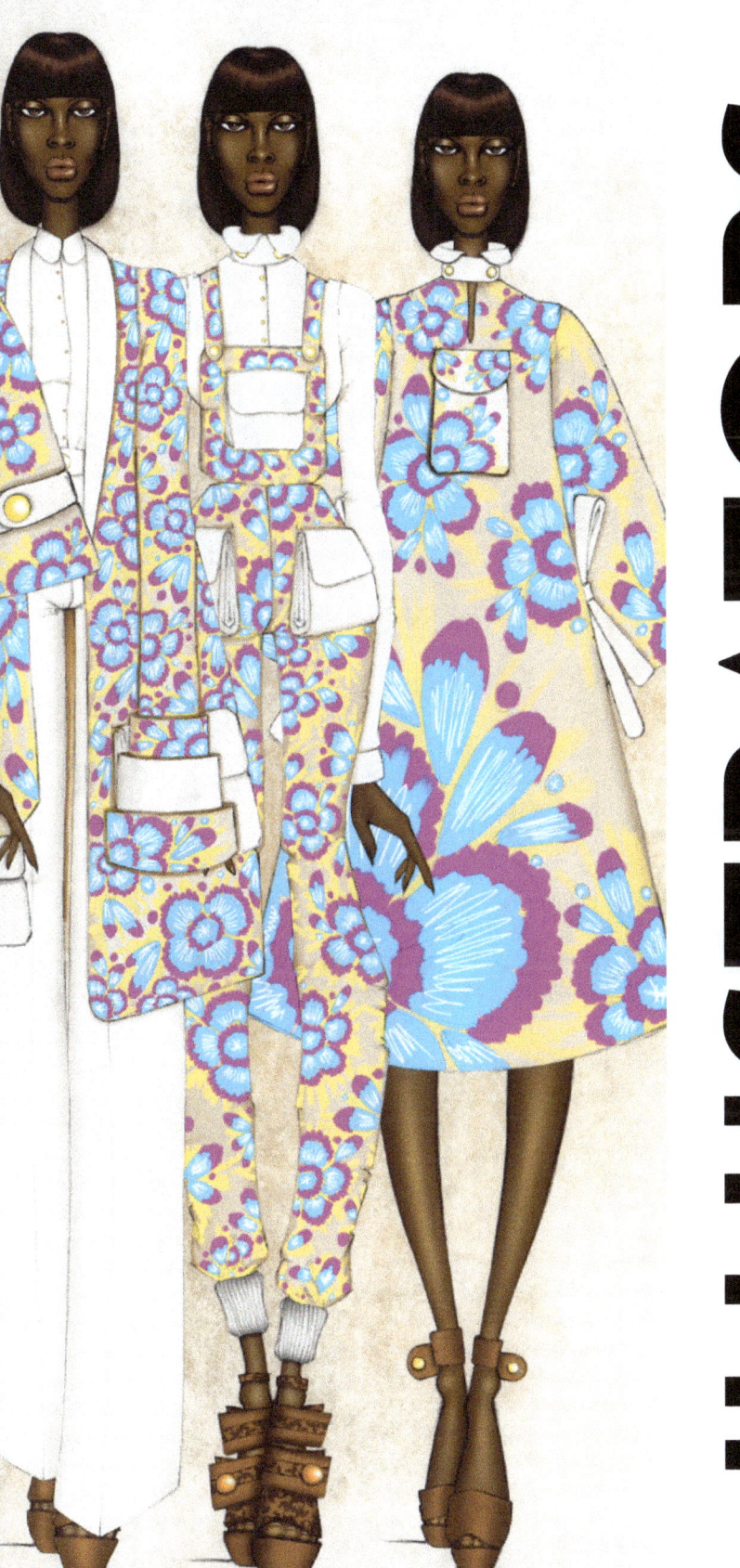

ILLUSTRATORS

This page: *Joggers*, digital Illustration, 2015

Opposite: *Untitled*, digital Illustration, 2015

'My fashion illustrations are my alter egos … at least if I can't wear the clothes, I can very well draw them.'
Adesola Lasisi

ADESOLA LASISI

A fine and applied art graduate, Adesola Lasisi turned to fashion illustration whilst studying for a master's degree. Introduced to the discipline courtesy of social media, namely Instagram, Lasisi cites the work of leading fashion illustrators on the platform for sparking her interest. Fashion illustration enables Lasisi to combine her love of fashion with her formal art training and is a form of self-expression, a vehicle to render her figures in the clothes she can imagine herself wearing. The resulting aesthetic is a journey through the wardrobe of the everyday girl who is contemporary and stylish in her outlook. Lasisi primarily works with marker pens, but has begun experimenting with digital illustration. Living and working in Lagos, Nigeria, Lasisi is part of an emerging generation of illustrators whose work is enabling a growing awareness of fashion illustration, giving it a greater significance in the local industry.

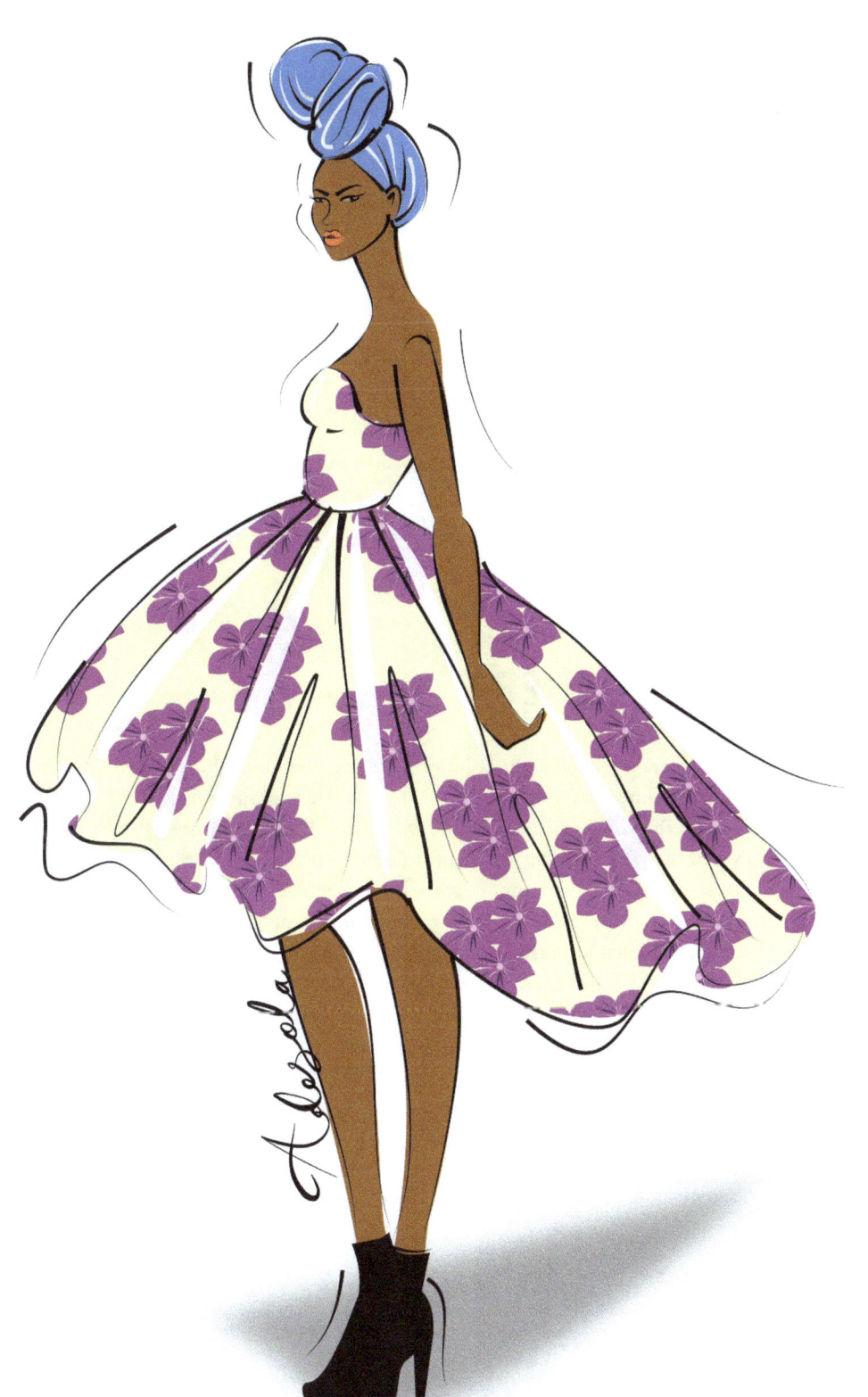

'My style is feminine, bold …
evoking emotion.'

Claire Idera

CLAIRE IDERA

Claire Idera is a self-taught fashion illustrator. She initially
studied architecture, but switched to fashion illustration halfway
through the course as she sought a way to combine a long-held
love of drawing with her passion for fashion. Idera's illustrations
juxtapose a delicate femininity with strong decisive lines and
splashes of bright, bold colour. Favouring mixed media, she
combines digital with traditional hand-drawing techniques,
mainly working with ink, watercolour, coloured pencils, marker
pens and acrylic paint. Idera divides her time between the UK
and Nigeria, where she runs workshops for budding fashion
illustrators. She sees her work as a complement to local Nigerian
fashion designers, and is driven by a need to work with them to
strengthen and help develop the industry as a whole. Pencil in
hand, Idera can often be spotted alongside the catwalks of Lagos'
Fashion Weeks, sketching styles as they come down the runways.

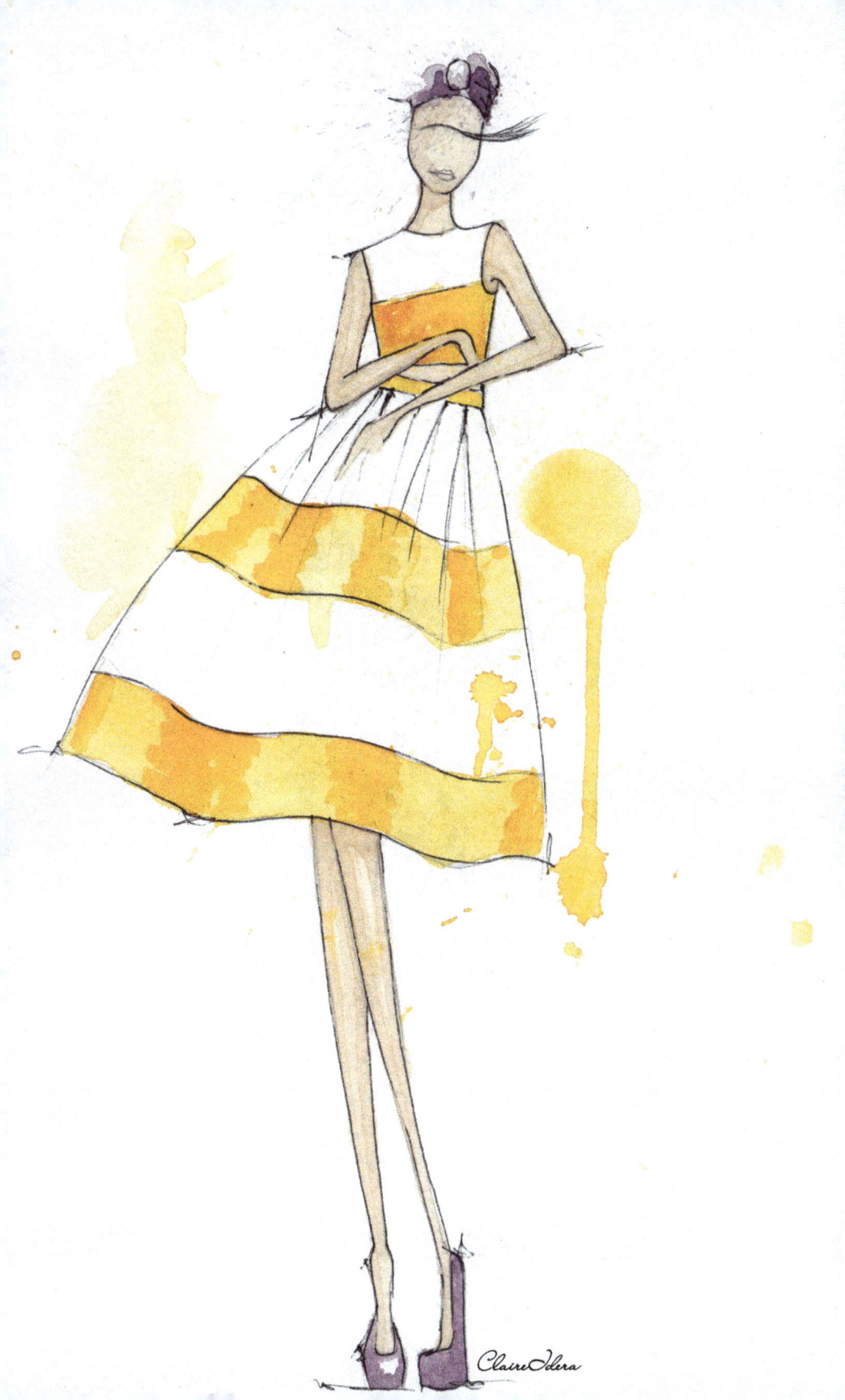

ClaireOdera

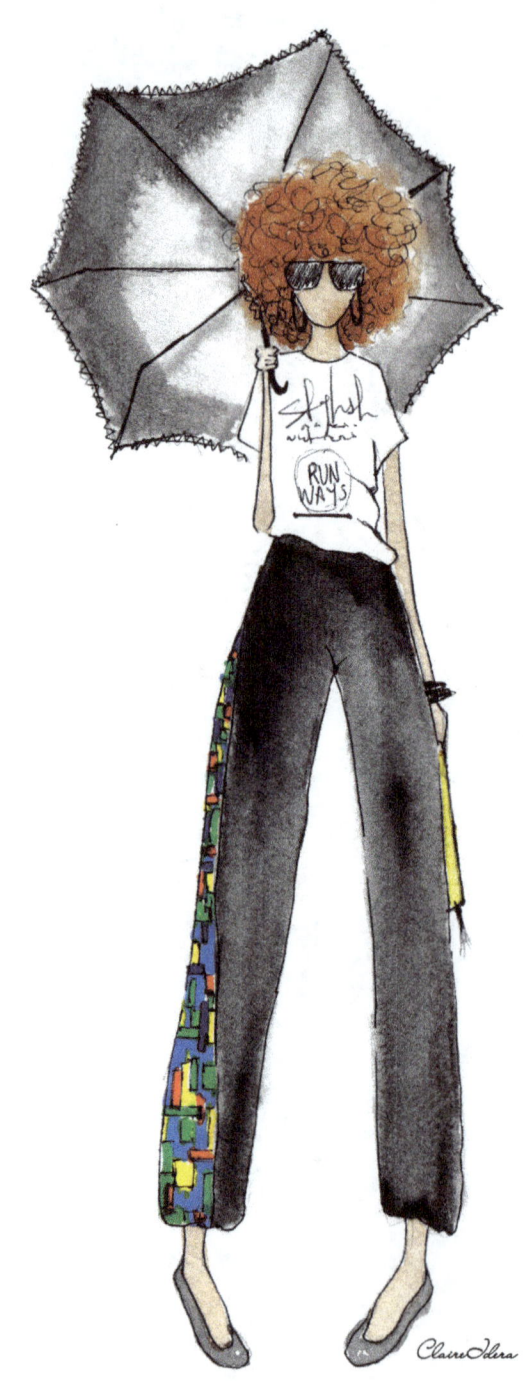

Stylish Girl, ink and watercolour, 2014

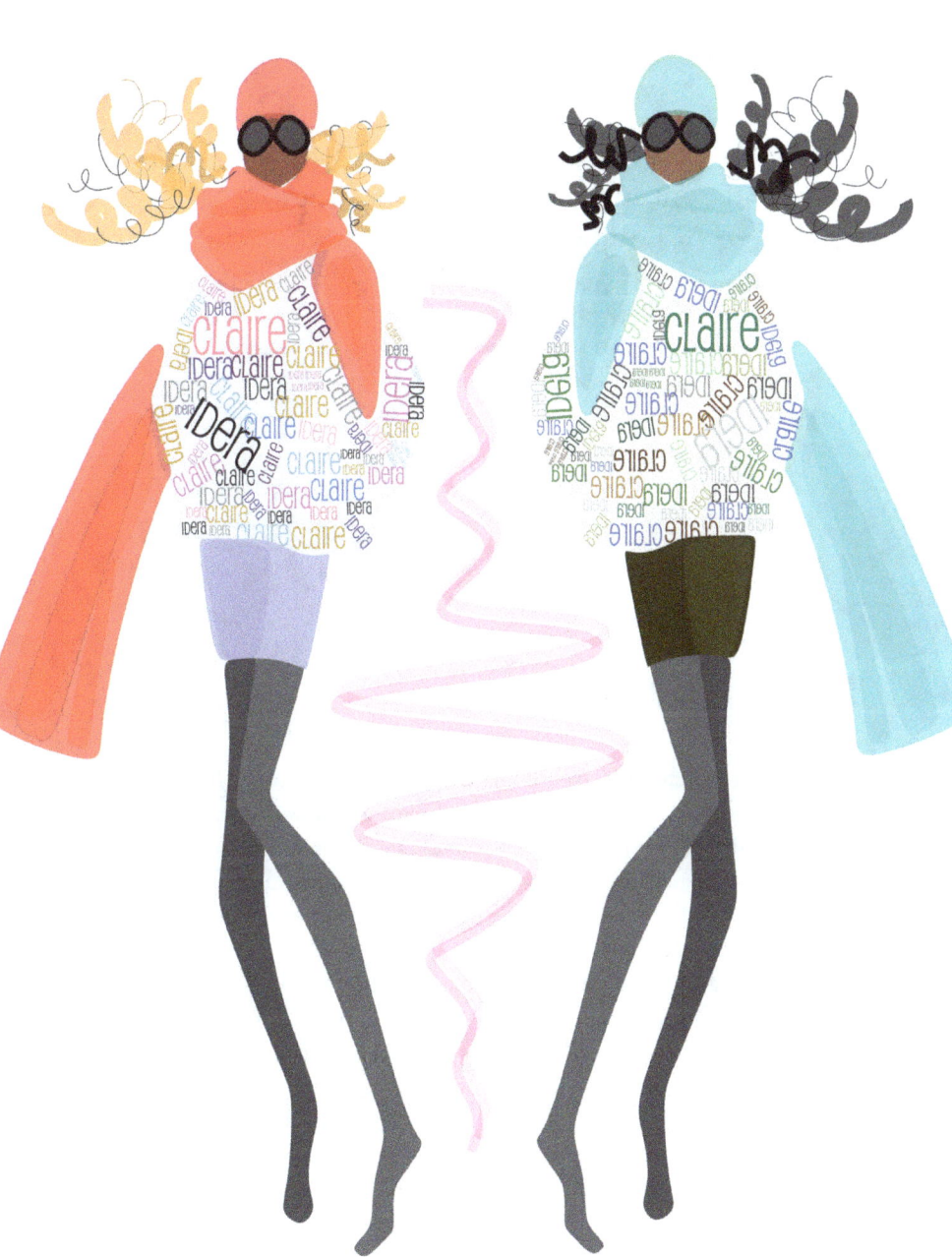

Untitled, digital illustration, 2013

'I love the rhythmic flow of the human
form and contours and enjoy sketching
it in the way I enjoy my favourite
meal. The dynamism is so amazing.'

Ibe Ananaba

IBE ANANABA

Nigerian art director, graphic designer, illustrator, and painter Ibe
Ananaba, has always been drawn to sketching the human body. He
first began illustrating fashion when friends approached him to
capture their ideas on paper to take to their local tailor. Ananaba
views fashion illustration as an exciting medium that introduces
new perspectives to interact with fashion, and as an alternative to
photographing fashion that allows for the injection of more colour,
character and soul. Ananaba's work is highly evocative; his paintwork
in particular has a luminous quality about it, the brushstrokes
conveying energy and movement as the fluid lines flow through
light and dark shadows to bring forth the images within. Ananaba
prefers pen and watercolour to digital, saying that traditional
mediums help to immerse him in the moment, taking him on an
adventure that connects with his senses. Ananaba often sketches with
ballpoint pen as doodles or finished pieces. He particularly enjoys
the challenge of working with watercolour, a medium he sees as
unpredictable, and therefore, exciting in relation to the end result.
He also works with acrylics, charcoals, marker pens and oil paint.

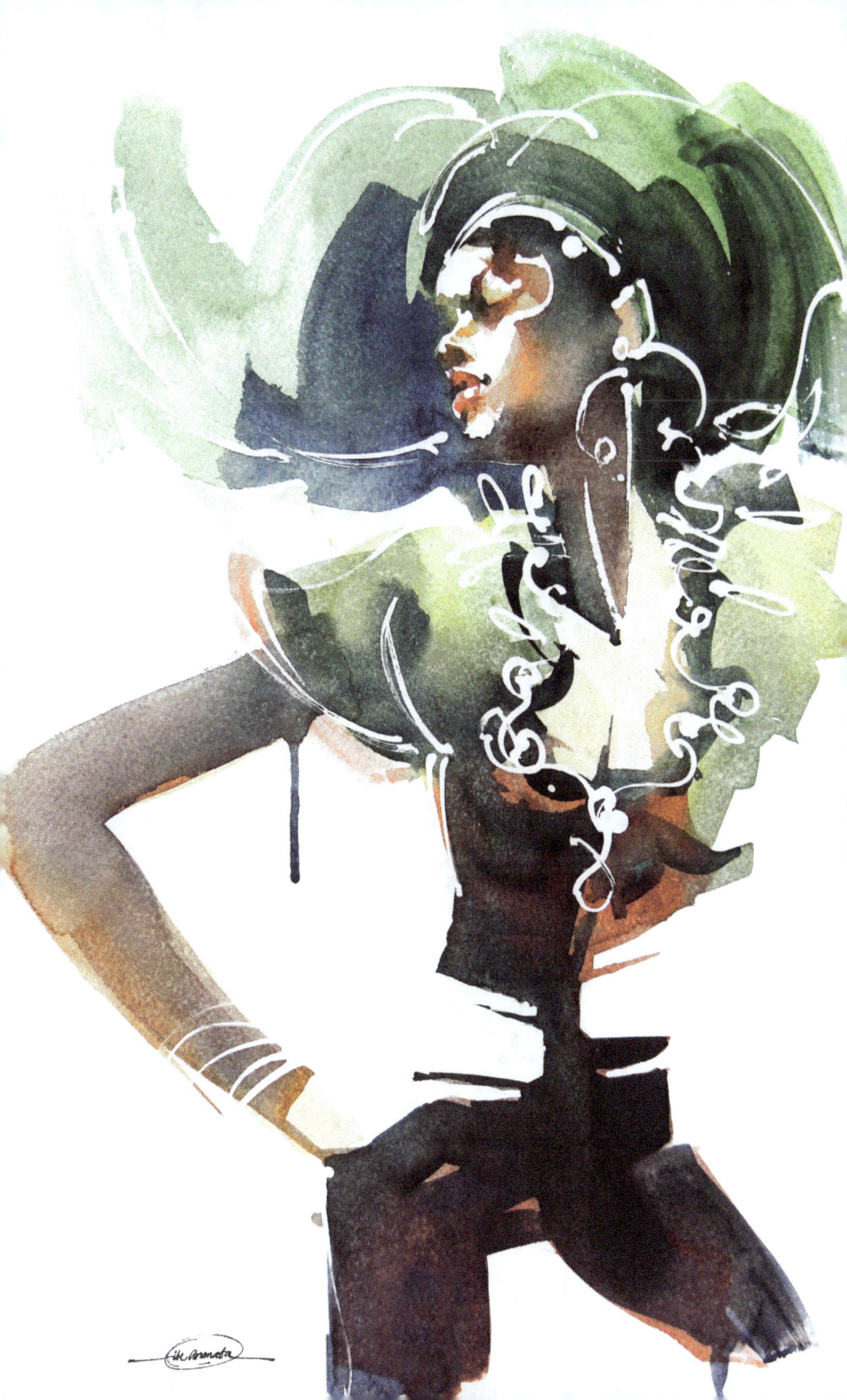

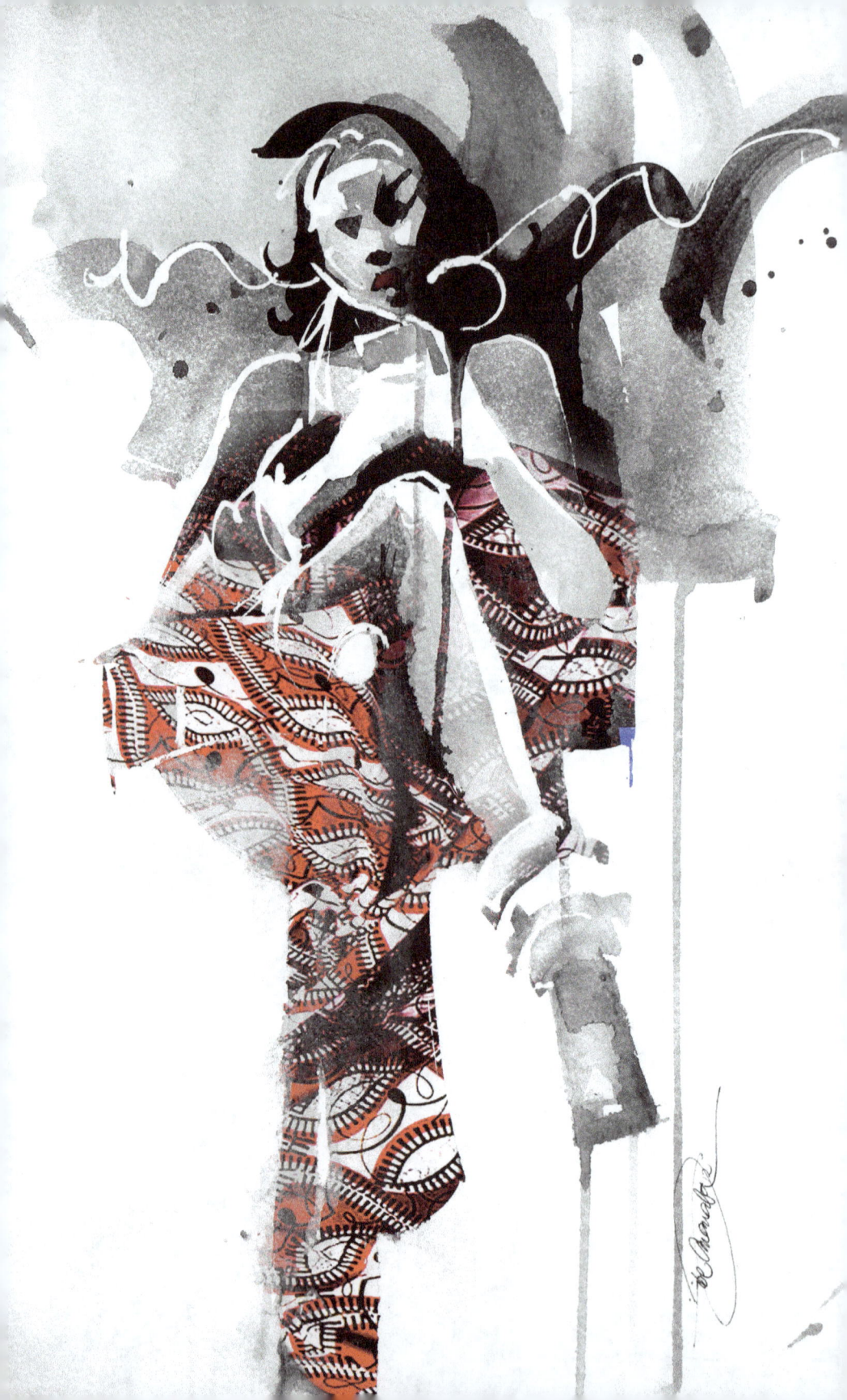

Opposite: *Status Update (2)*, mixed media (watercolour and Photoshop), 2012

This page: *Position of Power*, ink on paper, 2013

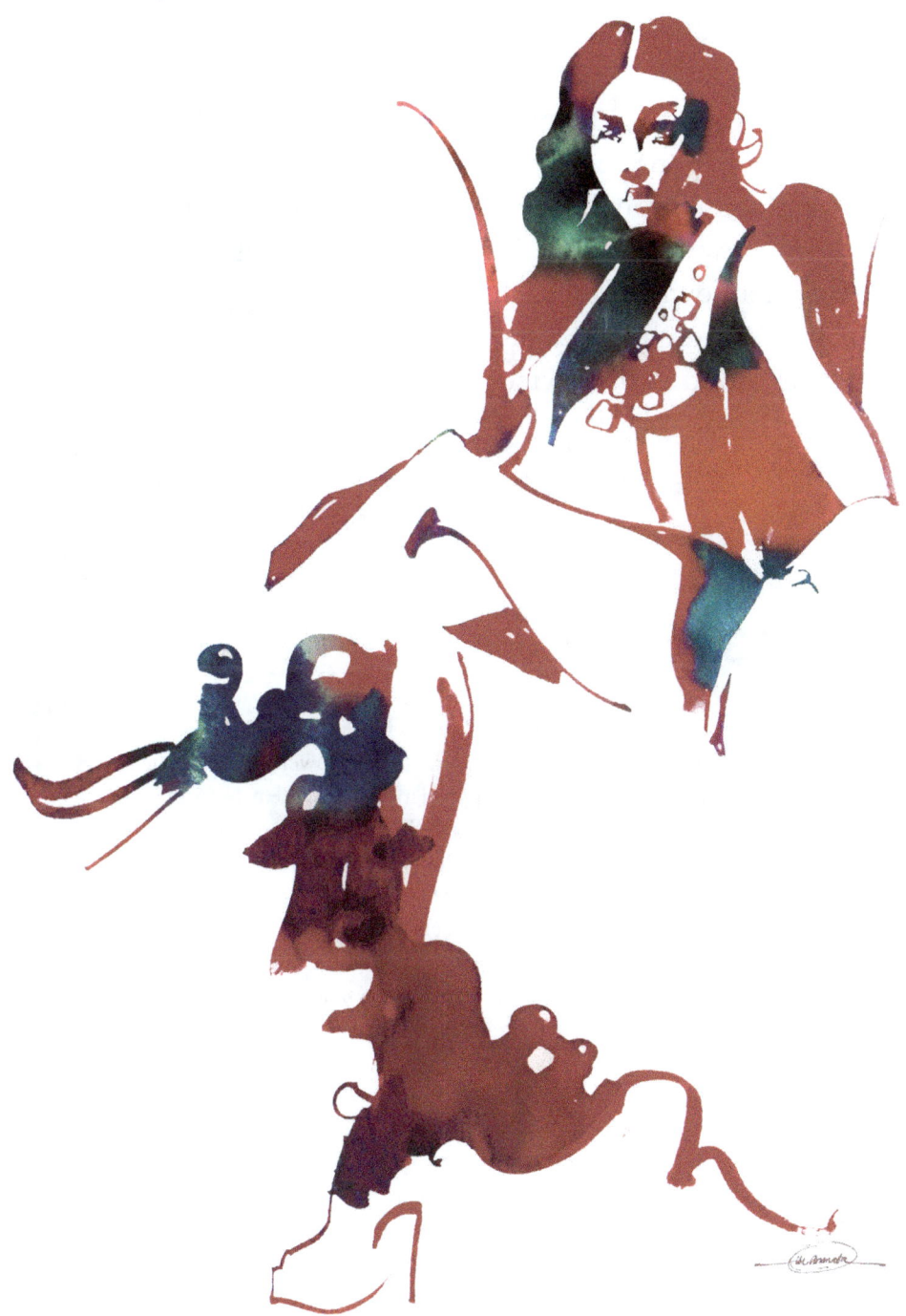

This page: *Thigh-High Ballet Boot*, colour pencil and marker pen, 2015

Opposite: *Sevyn Streeter*, colour pencil and marker pen, 2014

'I try, each time I put pen to paper, to represent what it is about women that I find powerful ... I focus on acknowledging each curve, each bend, each crease and each crevice of the female physique.'

Kobby Adu

KOBBY ADU

The term 'glamazon' comes to mind when first viewing Kobby Adu's illustrations, whose signature style depicts powerful, statuesque women, and is a reflection of his appreciation for the female form. Emotion, strong points of view, and the things he finds quirky and unique also influence Adu. Drawing, for Adu, is a form of therapy, a way to capture his thoughts and freeze moments in time, and he sees fashion illustration as a way to reach deep into the imagination and realize clothing and other designs that may not become a reality. Adu favours pen, coloured pencils, and felt-tip marker pens over pencil and digital art. He finds the permanence of pen particularly exciting, saying, 'With a pen, there's no turning back once you've made a wrong mark and there's something exciting about trying to make mistakes work to the benefit of the finished product.' Adu was born and raised in Accra, Ghana, and after a time in New York has returned home where he also works as an art director.

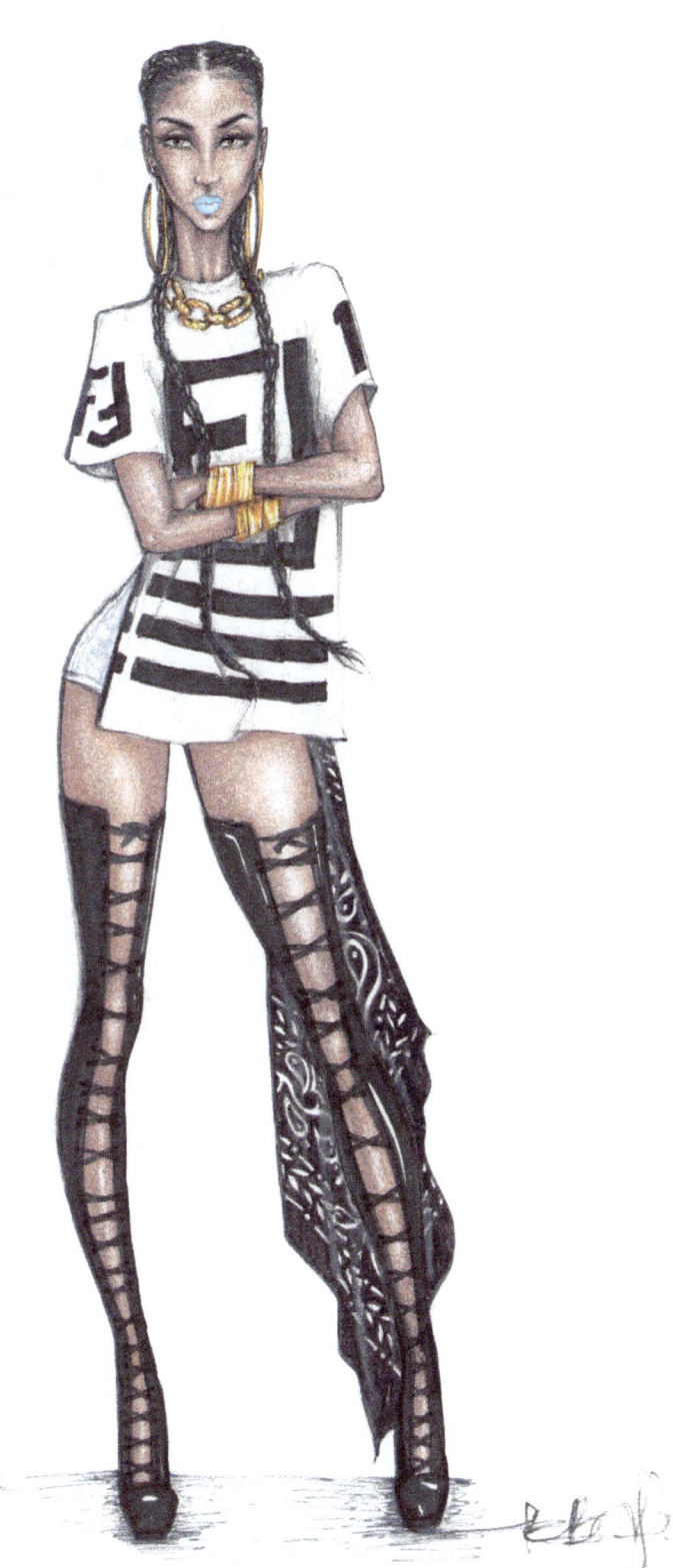

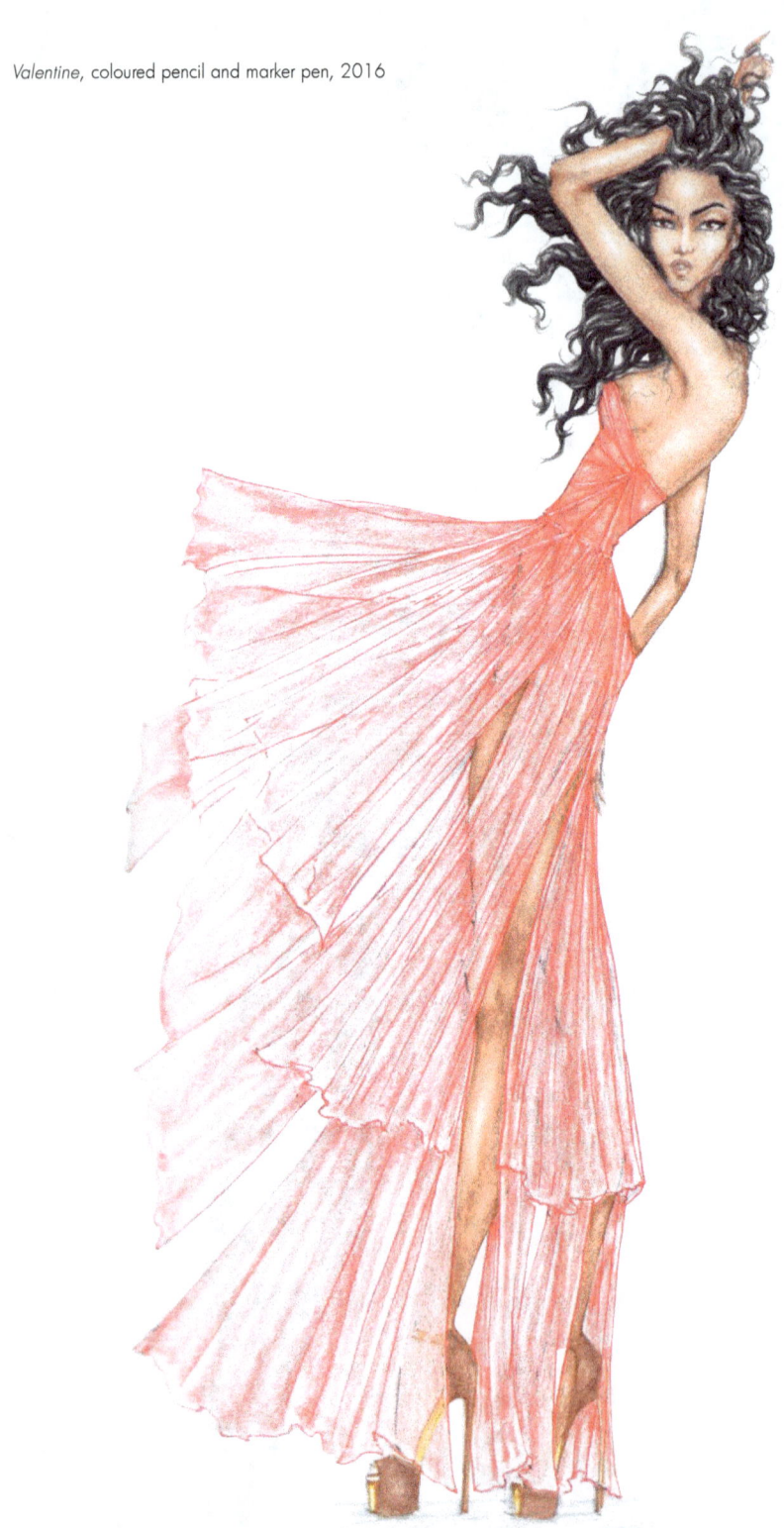

Valentine, coloured pencil and marker pen, 2016

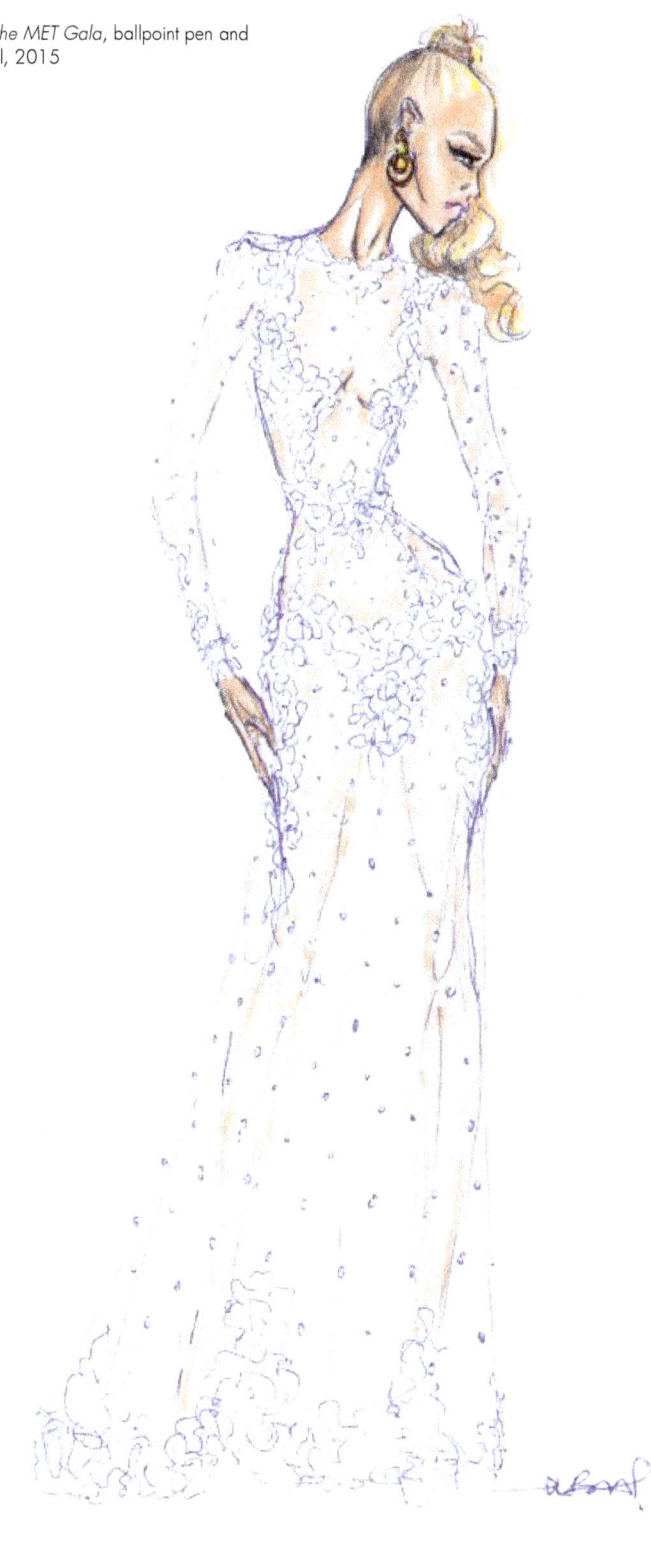

Bey by me at the MET Gala, ballpoint pen and coloured pencil, 2015

'I don't just sketch, I sketch
with passion and I want my
illustrations to tell the world that
creativity cannot be exhausted.'

Kyere Kwaku Awiti

KYERE KWAKU AWITI

Fashion illustration, for Kyere Kwaku Awiti, is about more than
just sketching figures and clothing. He uses his art as a way of
increasing awareness of the importance of the discipline in Ghana's
wider fashion industry, and is on a mission to become one of the
industry's greats. Awiti first became aware of fashion illustration as
a discipline whilst observing an illustrator friend at work. Carrying
out his own research and seeing the work of leading illustrators
only served to heighten his interest. Awiti's style focuses on the
garment rather than facial or figure details, which he sketches
in merely to give form to the clothing. He cites haute couture,
colour, blogs, animation and his environment as key sources of
inspiration, and prefers to work with a combination of what he calls
'dry media' – pen and coloured pencils – and computer graphics.

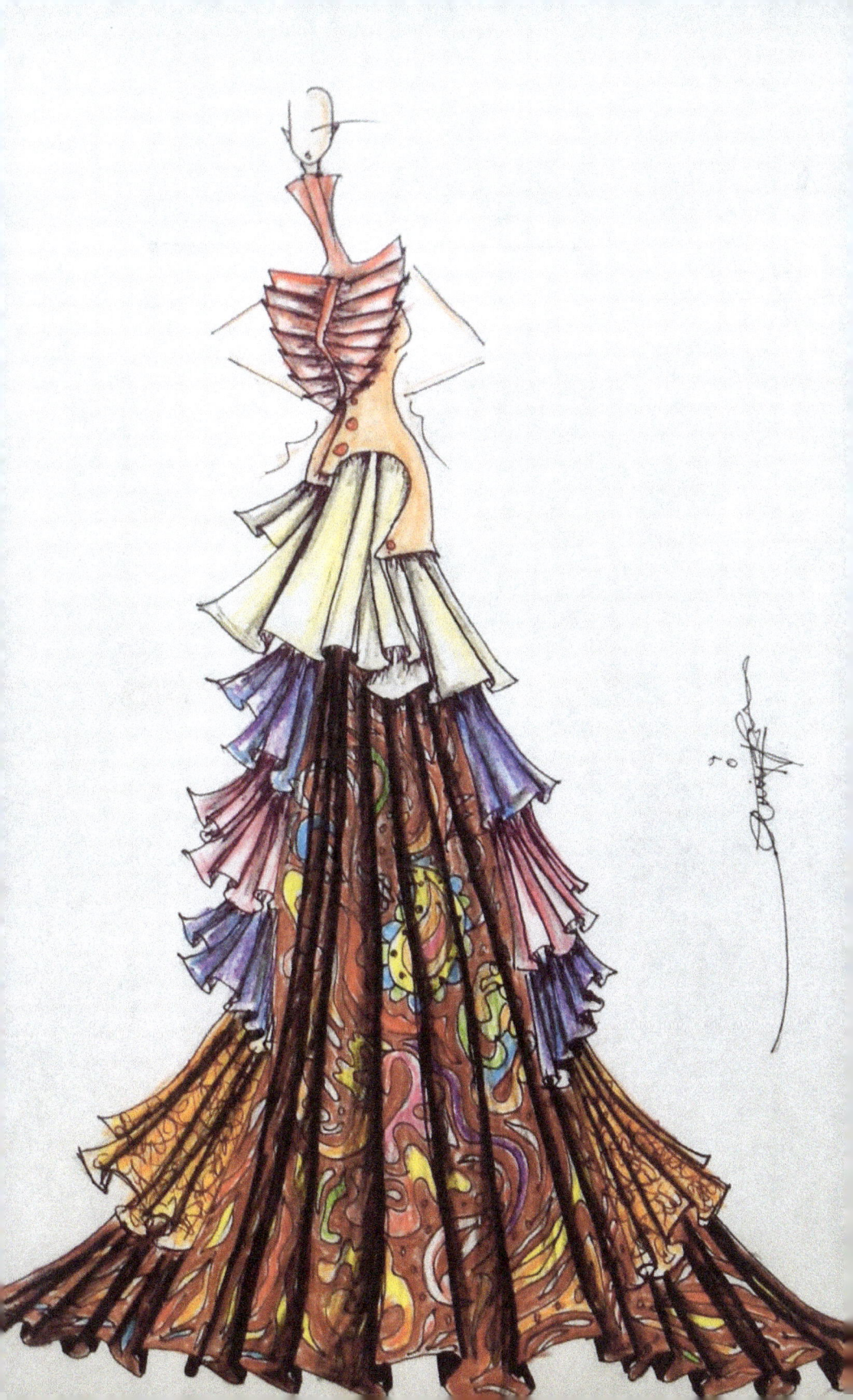

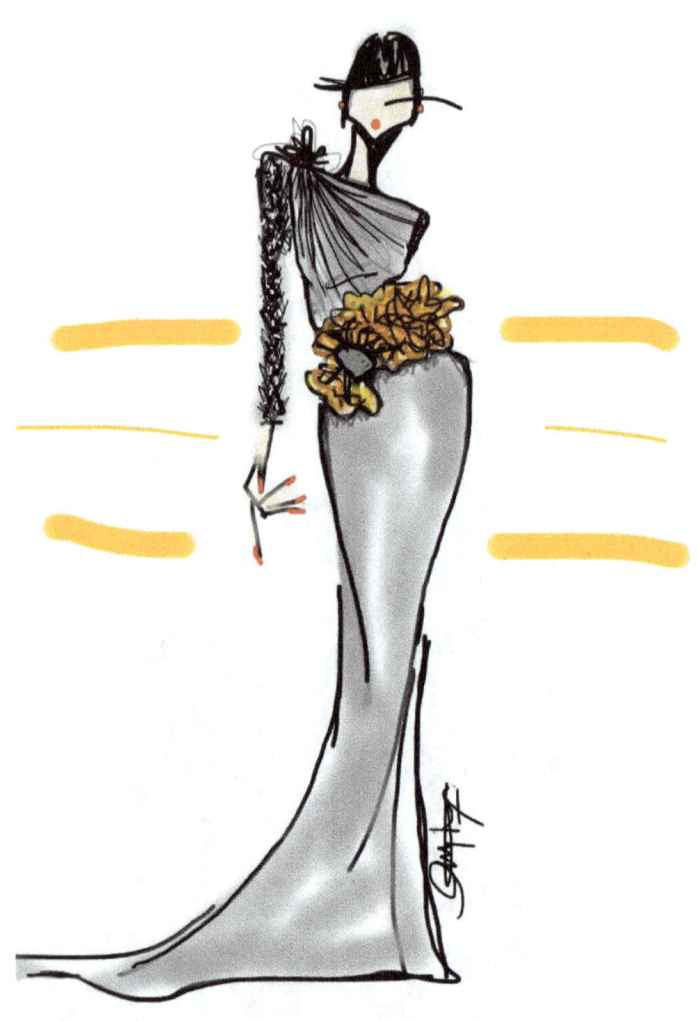

Mushroom Vibes, digital illustration, 2015

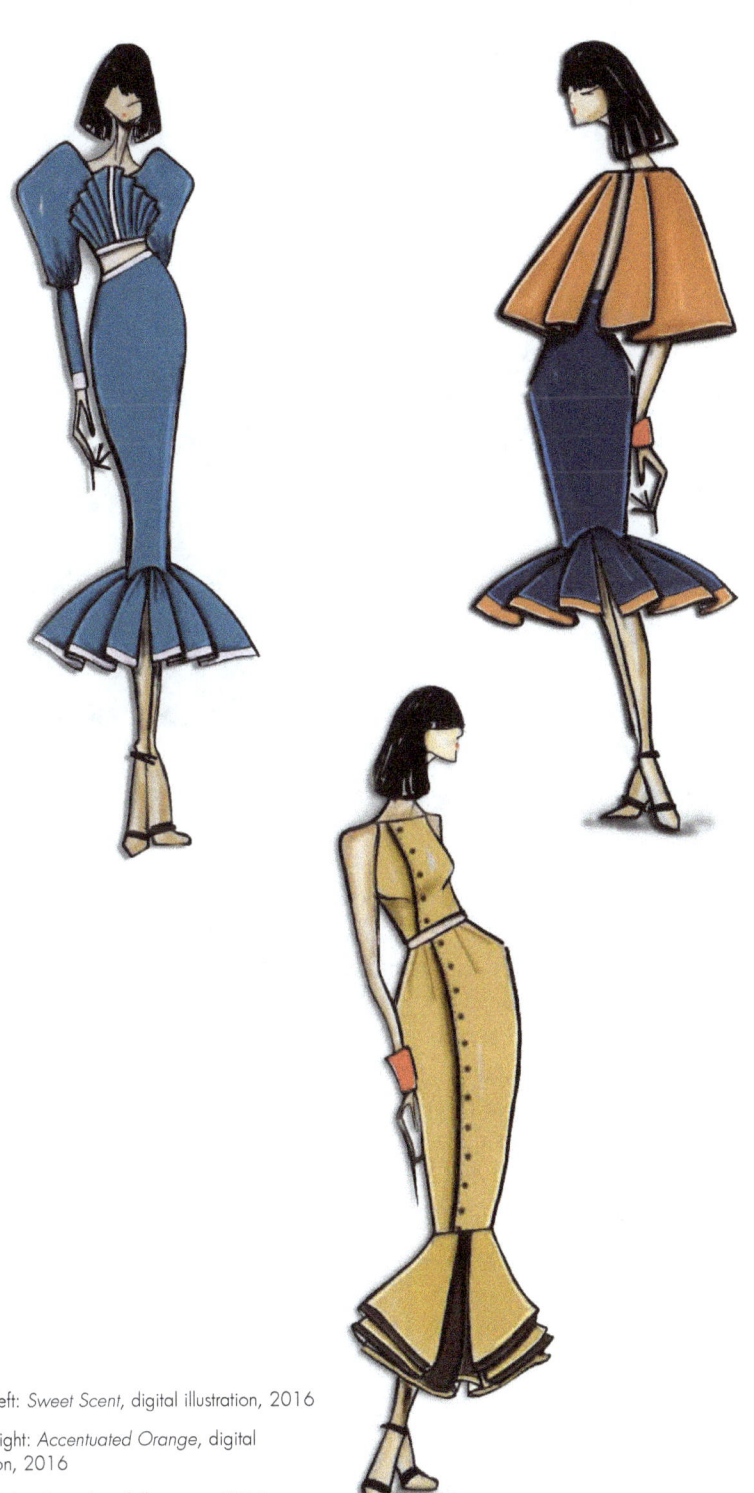

Above left: *Sweet Scent*, digital illustration, 2016

Above right: *Accentuated Orange*, digital illustration, 2016

Below: *Nostalgia*, digital illustration, 2016

This page: *LemyBeauty*, soft pastel and marker pen, 2016

Opposite: *Summer Cover Girl*, marker pen, coloured pencil and soft pastel, 2015

'I was so drawn to the beauty of this kind of art that I felt so inspired, motivated and driven to become what they [fashion illustrators] are.'

LeeAnn Visser

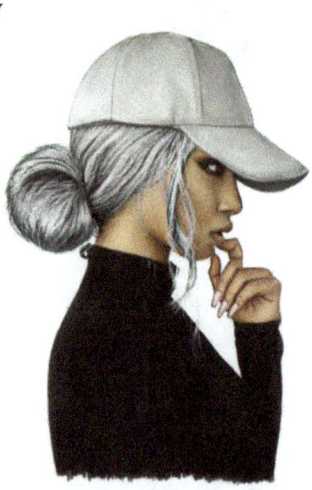

LEEANN VISSER

South African fashion illustrator LeeAnn Visser's career began after seeing the work of other illustrators on social media. Captivated by what she was seeing, Visser began creating, then posting her own illustrations on social media. Describing her style as bold, detailed, clean, trendy, softened and attention-grabbing, Visser's depictions of real and imagined figures are based on photorealism, her pens capturing minute details – from the tone of glowing tanned skin to the subtle highlights in strands of hair. Visser produces all her illustrations by hand, her preferred technique as she has found digital not to her liking. Soft pastels are Visser's favourite medium to work with, choosing them for the high level of blending ability and the smooth and soft effect they give to her illustrations.

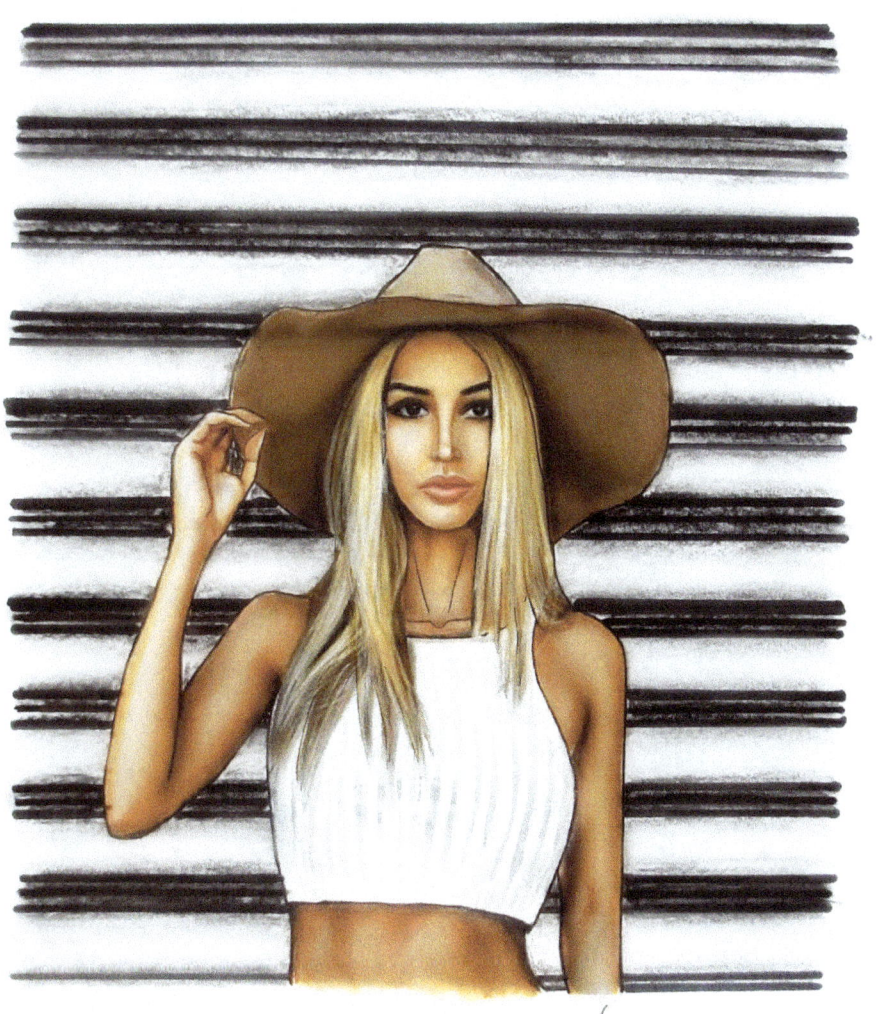

@leeannvisser

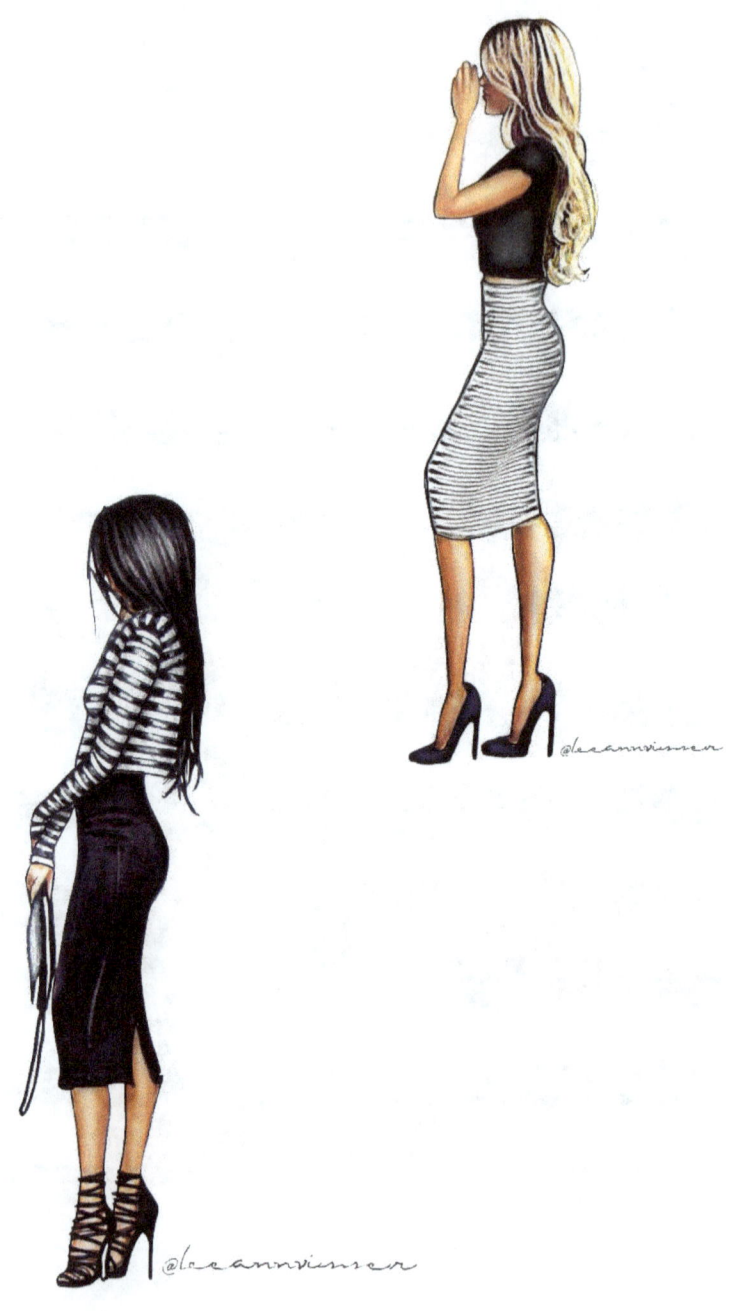

Above: *Chic Streetstyle*, marker pen and coloured pencil, 2015

Below: *Walk In Wonderland*, marker pen and coloured pencil, 2015

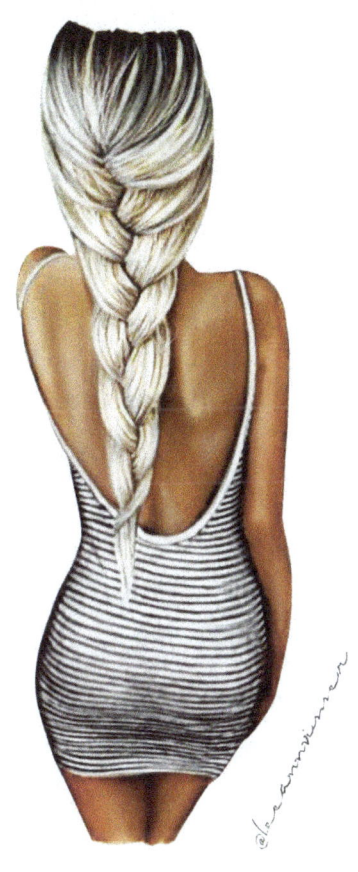

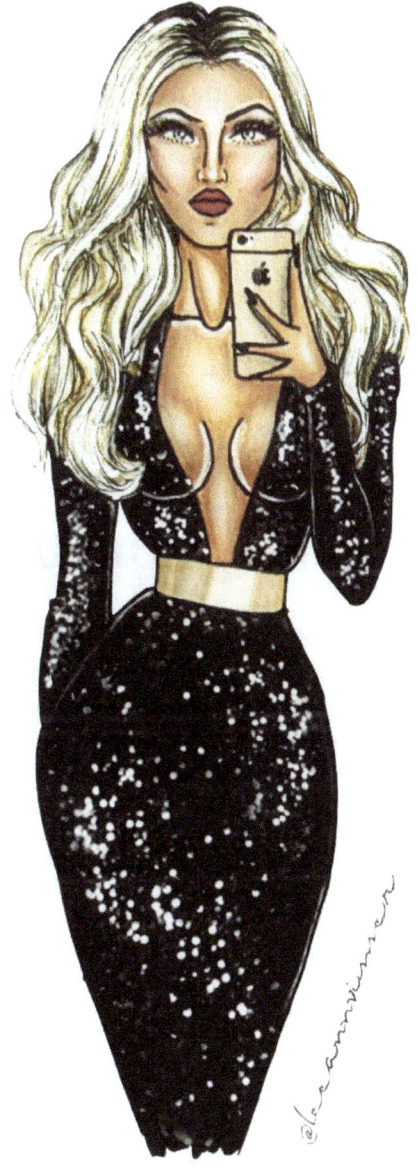

Above: *Emily-Rose*, soft pastel and marker pen, 2016

Below: *Glamorous Selfie*, marker pen and coloured pencil, 2015

'I appreciated drawing facial profiles
and figures of all types of people,
as I occasionally asked myself
whether or not people of colour
were represented well enough.'

Lindsay Dhludhlu

LINDSAY DHLUDHLU

As a child growing up in South Africa, Lindsay Dhludhlu would
illustrate figures and collect outfits from magazines, putting
together themed collages to create background settings to fit
the figures. Looking back, she reflects on this as her way of
desperately trying to create something new that would reflect
the reality of those she saw around her. Studying visual arts and
design at college was a starting point for Dhludhlu's interest in
illustrating in general. Her illustrations are based on both abstract
and real women from her everyday life. She primarily works
with acrylic, oil, watercolour and ink, which she combines with
digital illustration techniques. And, like many of her peers, social
media makes a mark on her work, evident in her use of digital
photographs that she then paints over for a contemporary take
on the art of fashion illustration evolving in the digital age.

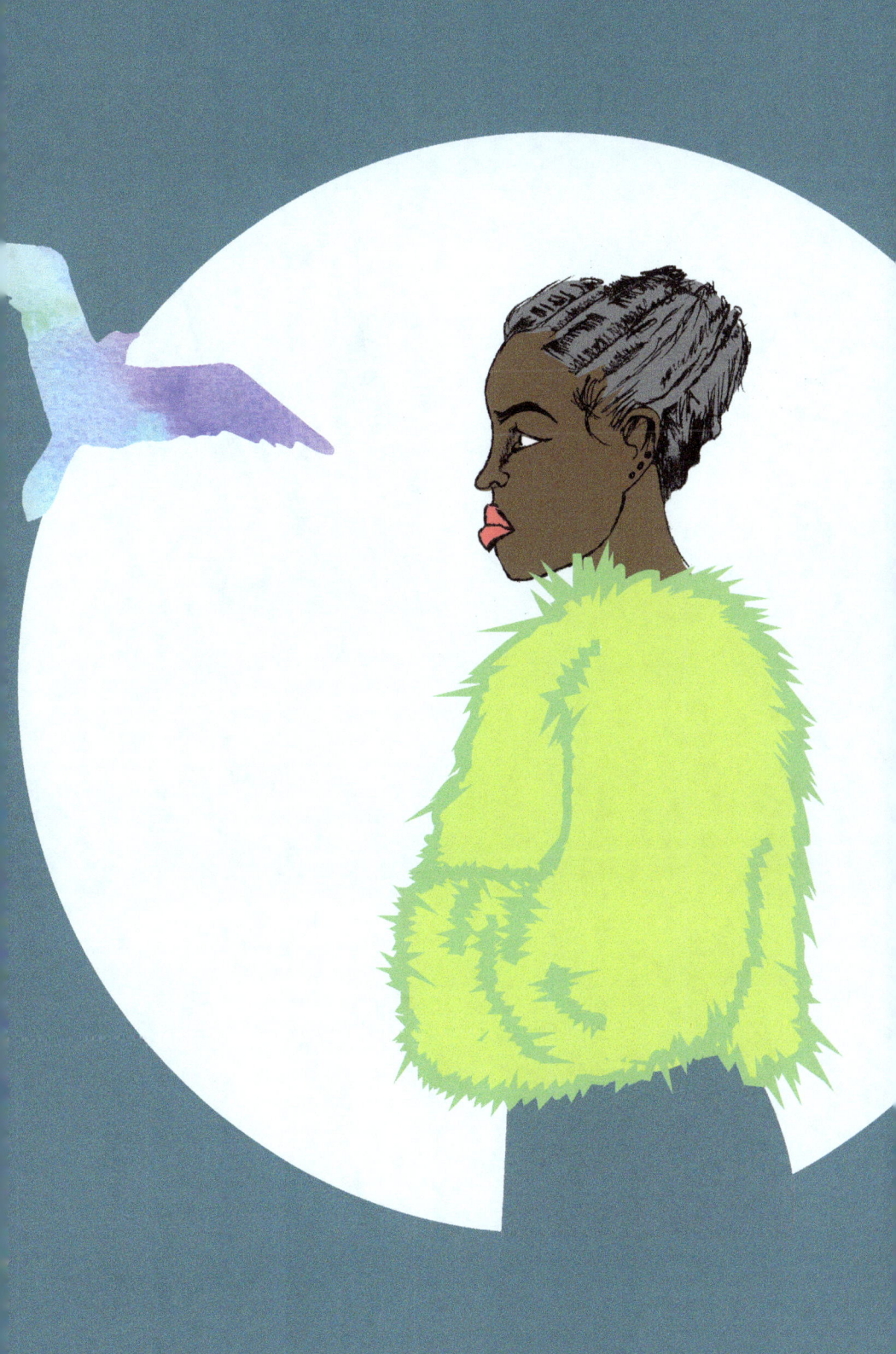

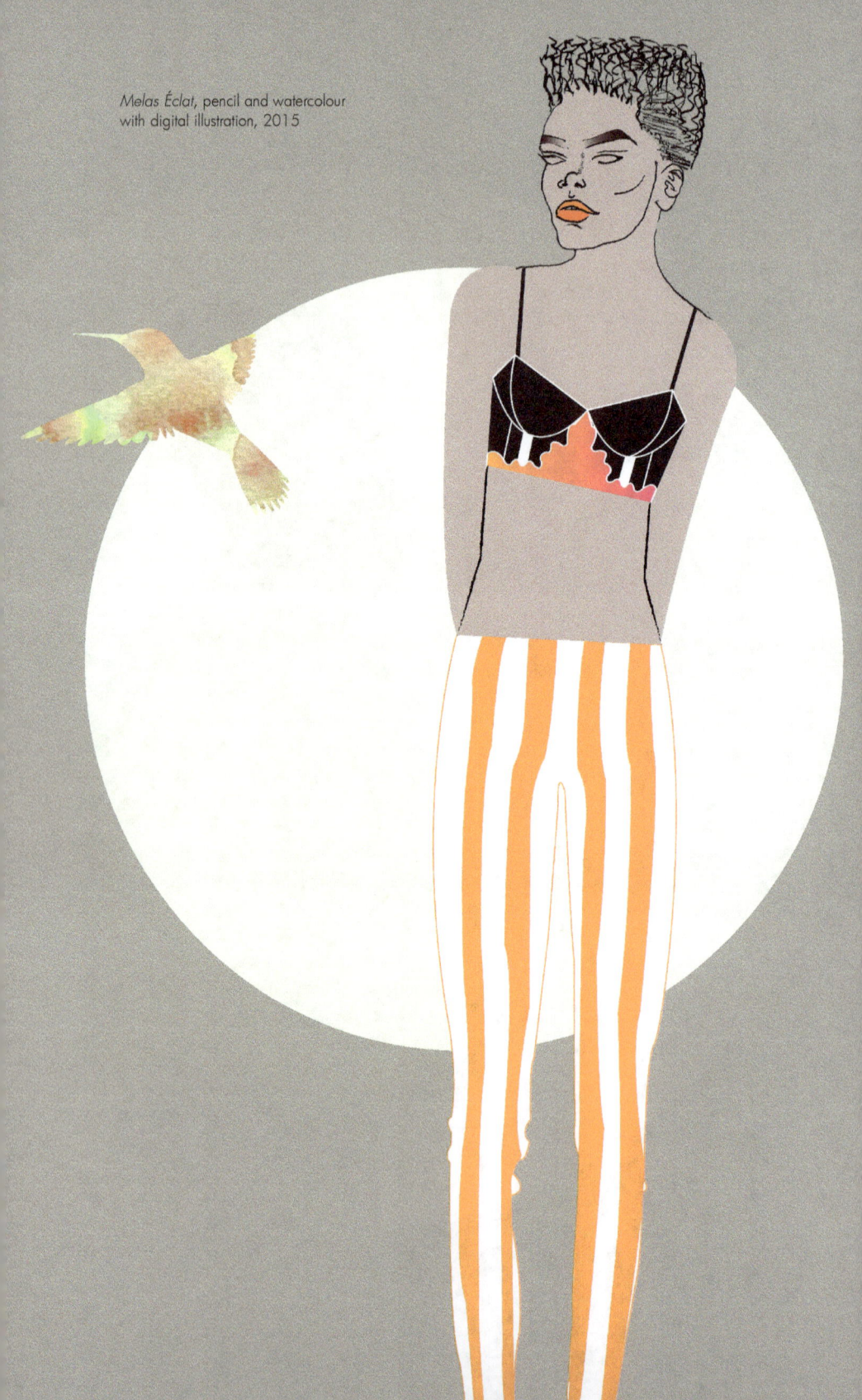

Melas Éclat, pencil and watercolour
with digital illustration, 2015

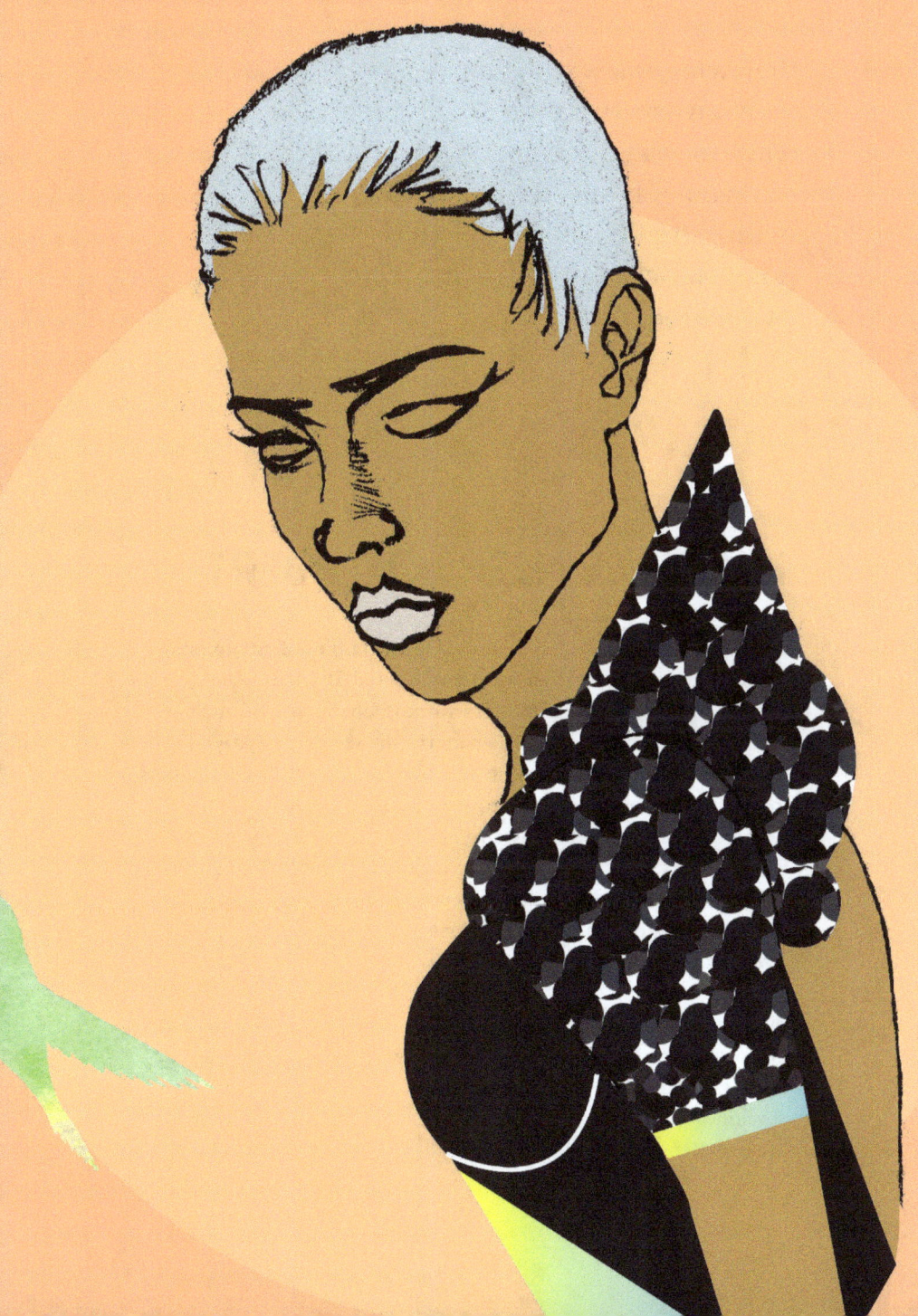

Beaute tour de force, pencil and watercolour with digital illustration, 2015

'Drawing is a way for me to start my creative process ... I get engrossed in designing prints and can endlessly spend time playing with scale, design and colour. I can get locked in for hours!'

Michelle Njeri Cuthbert

MICHELLE NJERI CUTHBERT

Michelle Njeri Cuthbert is a London-based fashion illustrator and textile designer. She studied textiles at Central St. Martins and Chelsea College of Art. Cuthbert's work is vibrant, playful and fashion-forward, inspired by the patterns she sees in everyday life. Her illustrations start out as line drawings in pen, which she transfers to a computer to add her signature bold, bright colours, mindful not to over stylize or computerize her illustrations as she feels this will lose the creative vision and the human element behind them. Cuthbert's work is also a vehicle to portray a message or story about life, create humour, or help bring awareness to the issues of others. She occasionally tinges her work with a political and serious edge, a nod to a time growing up in Kenya where she recalls spending Sunday afternoons tracing over the political cartoons in the local paper. Cuthbert continually draws inspiration from Kenya, notably seen in 'The Art of Carrying', an illustrative series she developed during a visit back to Kenya, where she pays homage to local women carrying their heavy loads whilst embracing style.

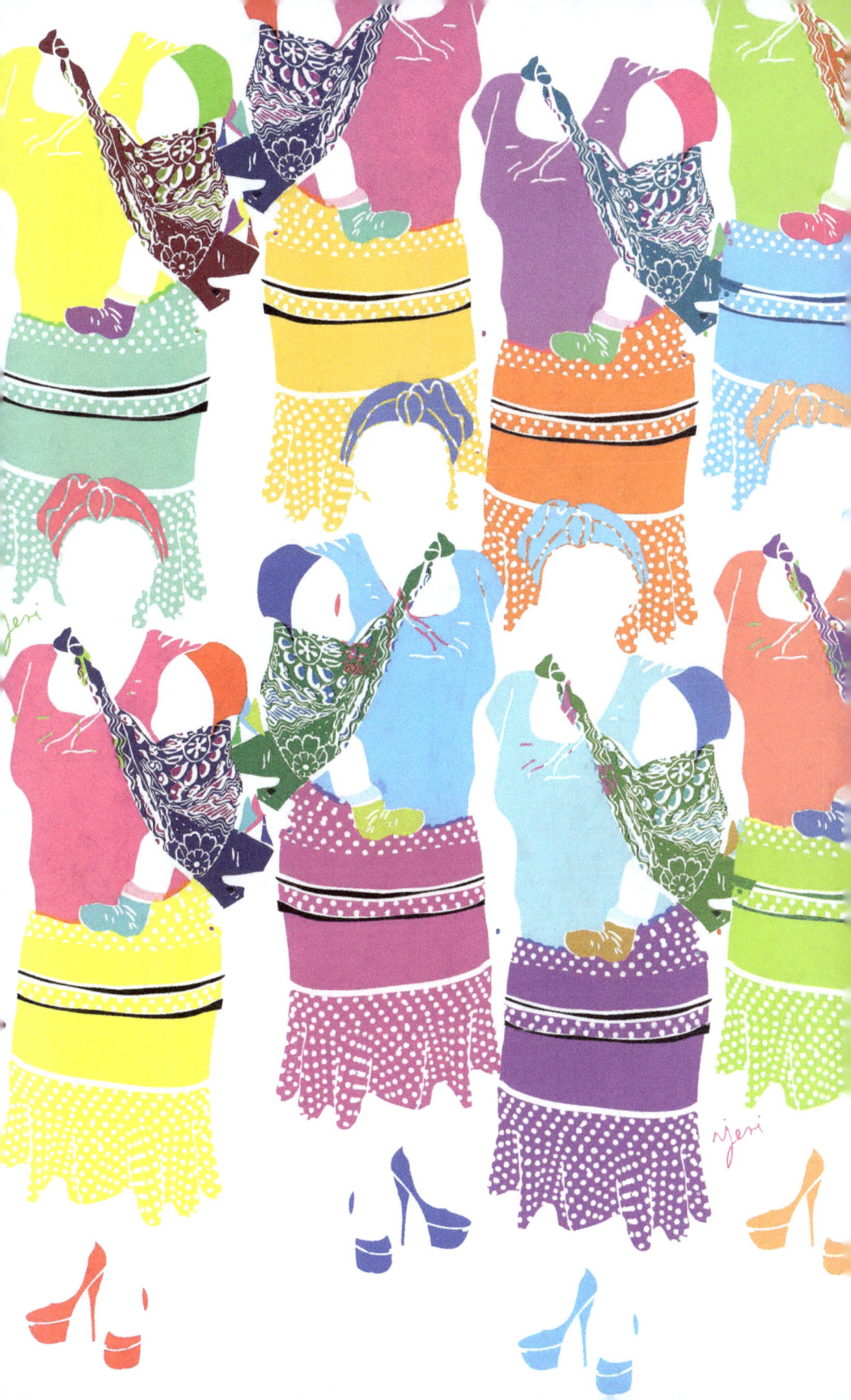

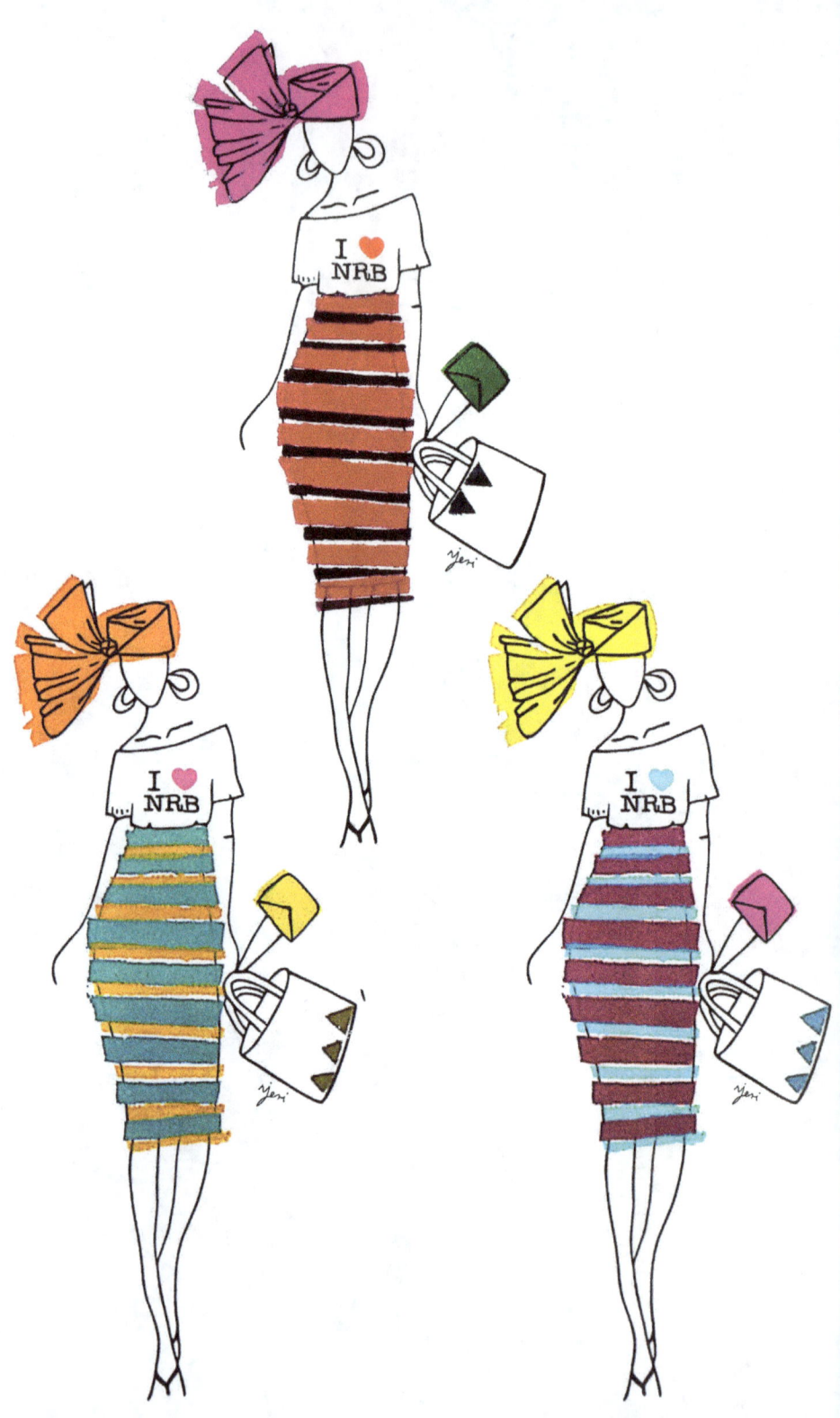

44

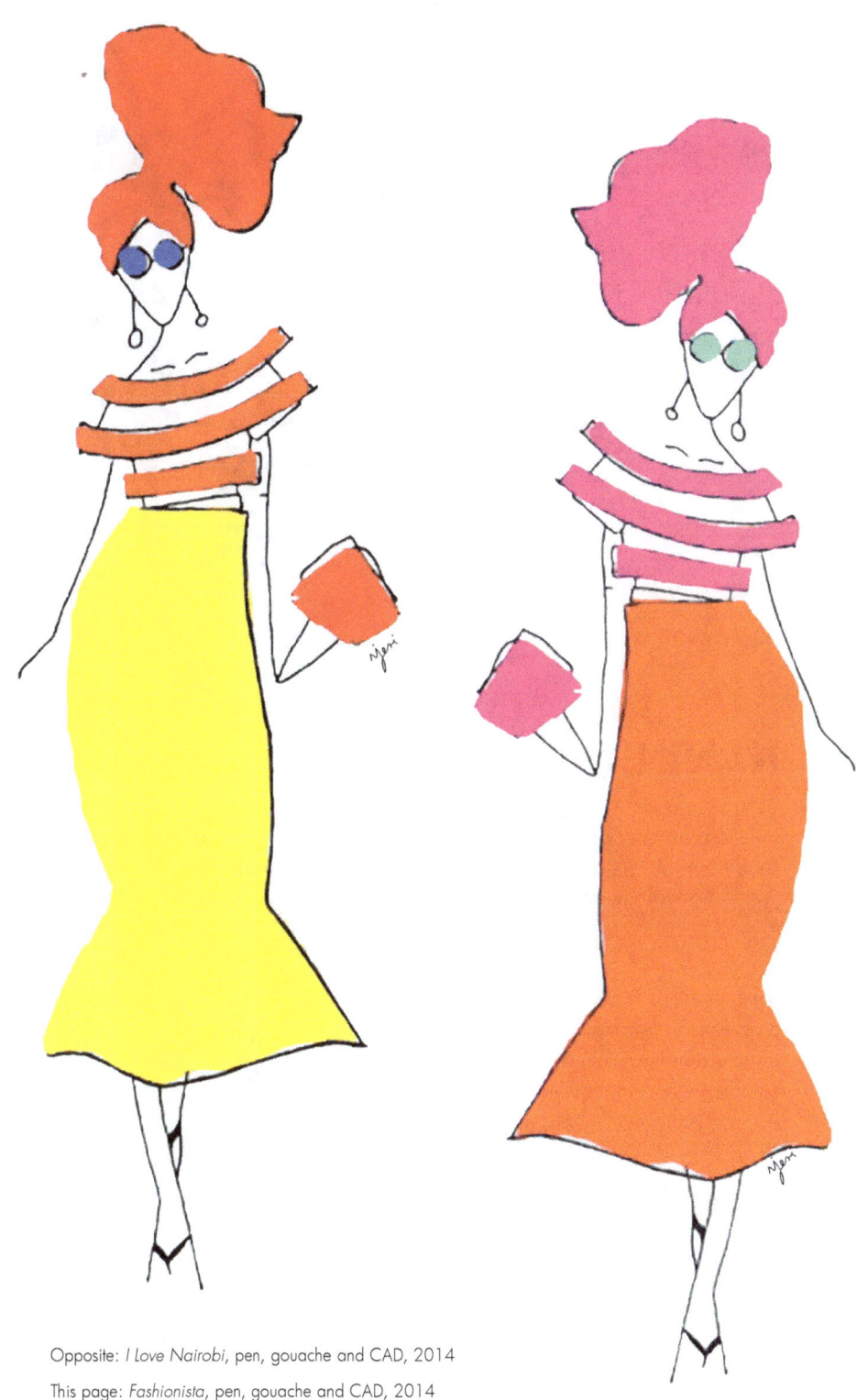

Opposite: *I Love Nairobi*, pen, gouache and CAD, 2014

This page: *Fashionista*, pen, gouache and CAD, 2014

Above: Curves, pen and marker pen, 2015
Below: *Khoza*, pen and marker pen, 2015

'When creating an illustration, I don't usually have a particular style in mind, because that usually limits me, creatively.'
Nanini

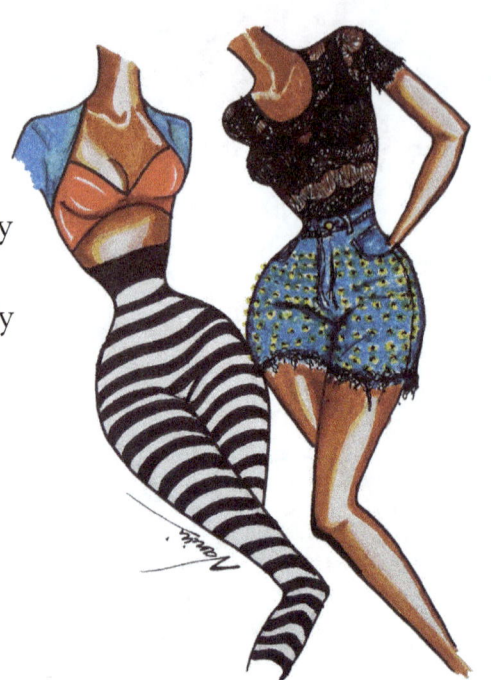

NANINI

June Nanini Wambua, known as 'Nanini', is a fashion illustrator from Nairobi, Kenya. Her interest in the discipline began unintentionally in 2014, having graduated with an accounting degree and realizing she had little passion for it. Unaware that one could make a living as a fashion illustrator, a chance act of copying an image from a fashion magazine and posting it to her Instagram page where it garnered more attention than all her other posts led her on a mission of discovery toward a new passion and the founding of NaninisArtDesigns. Nanini's illustrative style favours realism over abstract stylistic interpretations, and responds to a diverse pool of motivation and inspiration that ranges from leading social figures to nature and more. She mainly uses pen and marker pen, finding these mediums easier to work with than digital.

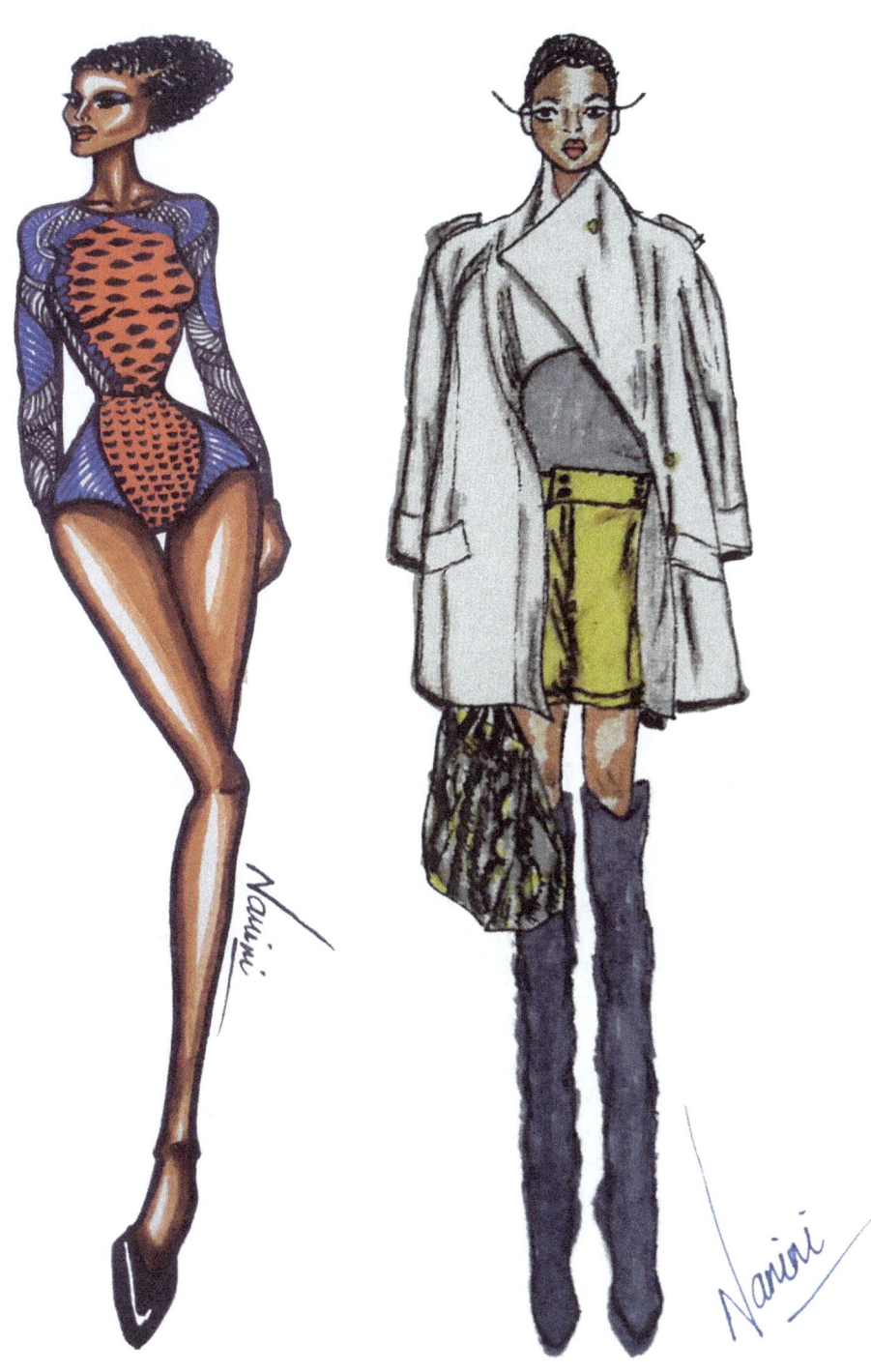

Left: *Scales*, pen and marker pen, 2015

Right: *Monday*, pen and marker pen, 2015

'As obsessed as I am with lines, drawing with a pen or pencil helps me to maintain a certain accuracy in my drawings.'
Nathaniel Adjei Bio

NATHANIEL ADJEI BIO

Ghanaian fashion illustrator Nathaniel Adjei Bio has always dabbled in drawing figures and clothing, but it was not until his high school years that fashion illustration became an outlet for him to showcase his talent and meet new people. Bio's work draws on several key sources of influence. He is heavily inspired by Surrealism, connecting to the liberated, no-rules nature of the movement. And his interest in the shapes and lines of architectural forms fuels a self-confessed obsession with creating straight, clean lines. Both of these sources of inspiration are reflected in his work through the exaggerated linear forms of his figures, mostly rendered in pen and ink on paper. Bio prefers this 'conventional' way of illustrating, as he feels it gives him more control, particularly when it come to drawing lines, but he does not rule out working with digital in the future.

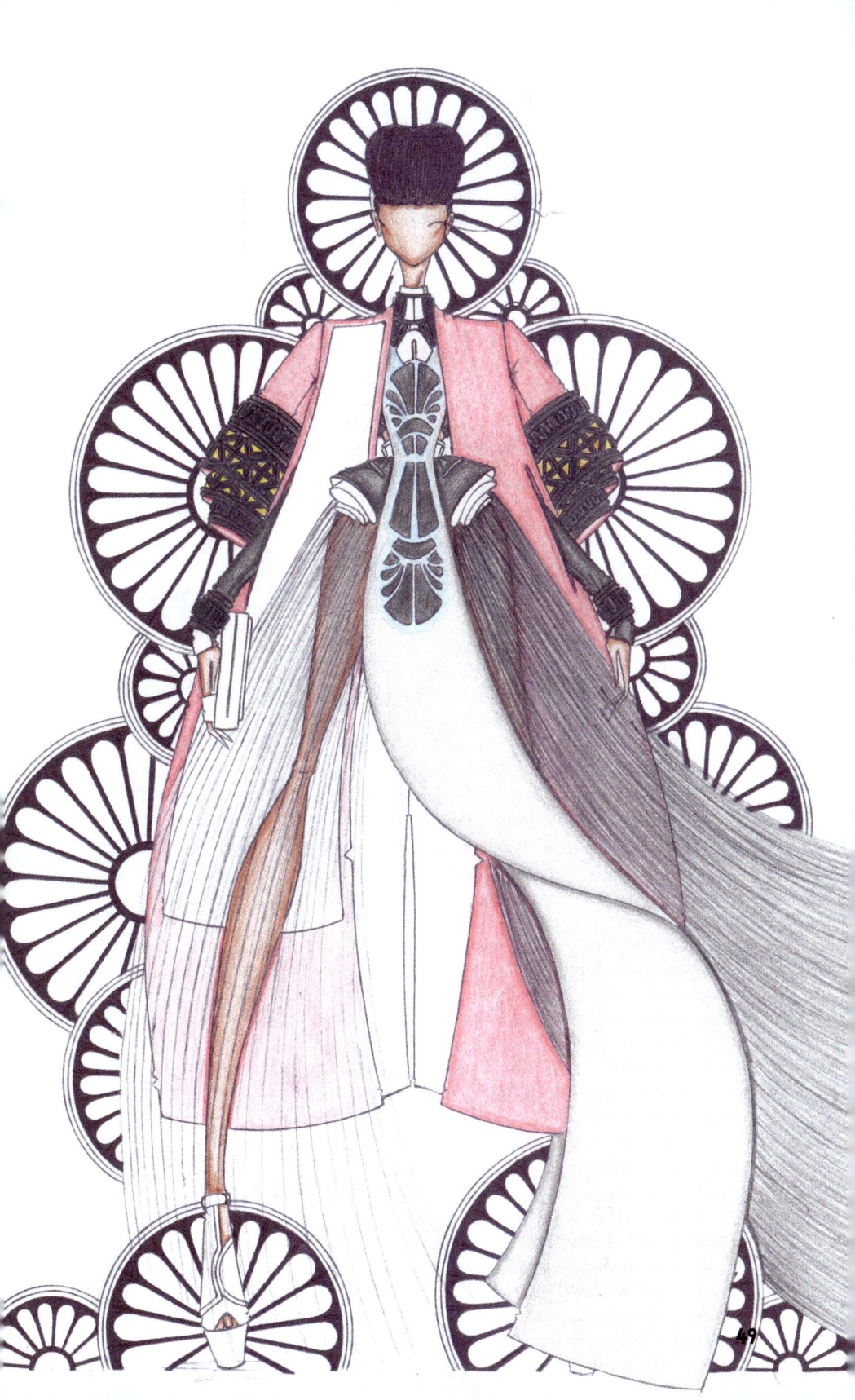

49

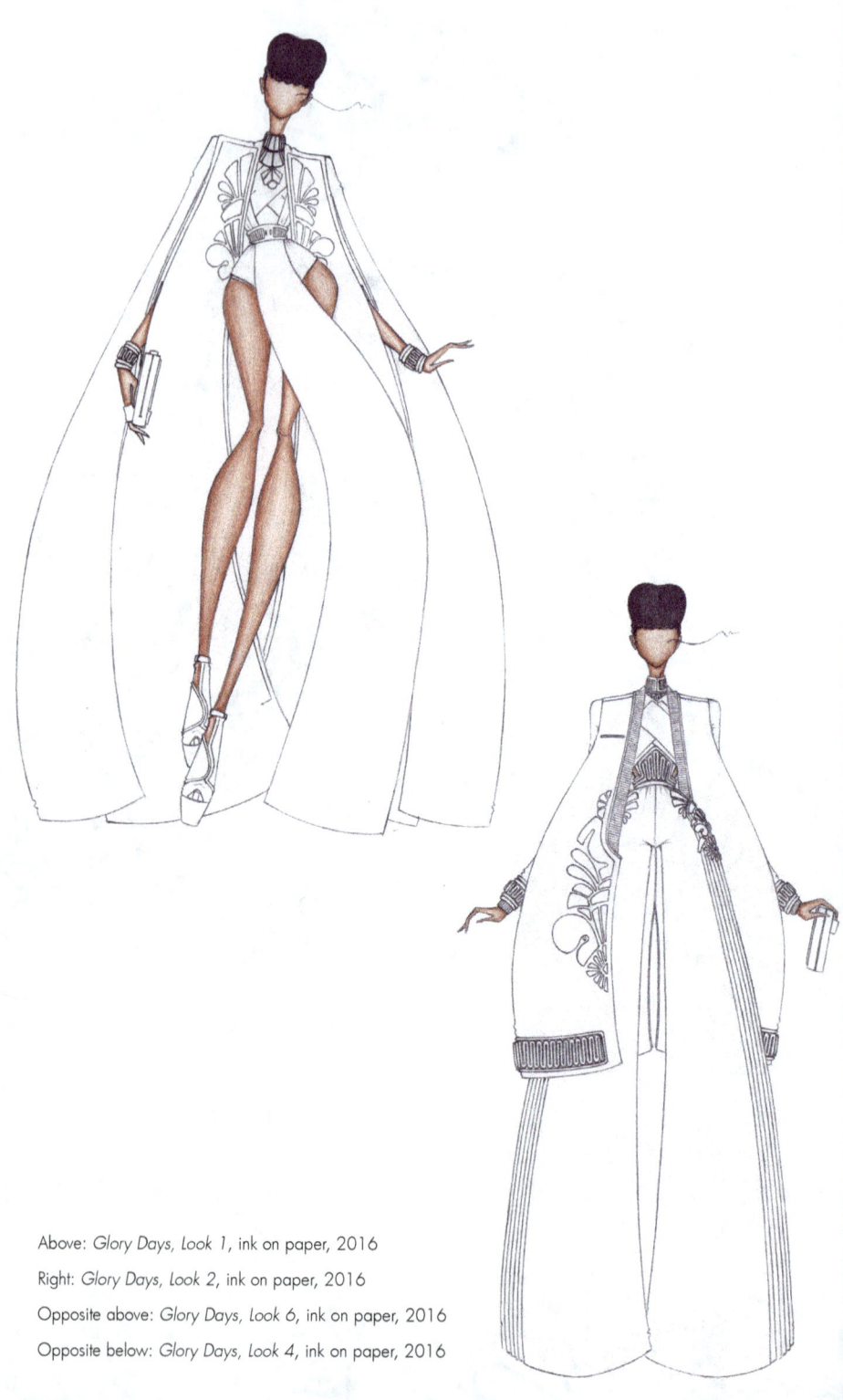

Above: *Glory Days, Look 1*, ink on paper, 2016

Right: *Glory Days, Look 2*, ink on paper, 2016

Opposite above: *Glory Days, Look 6*, ink on paper, 2016

Opposite below: *Glory Days, Look 4*, ink on paper, 2016

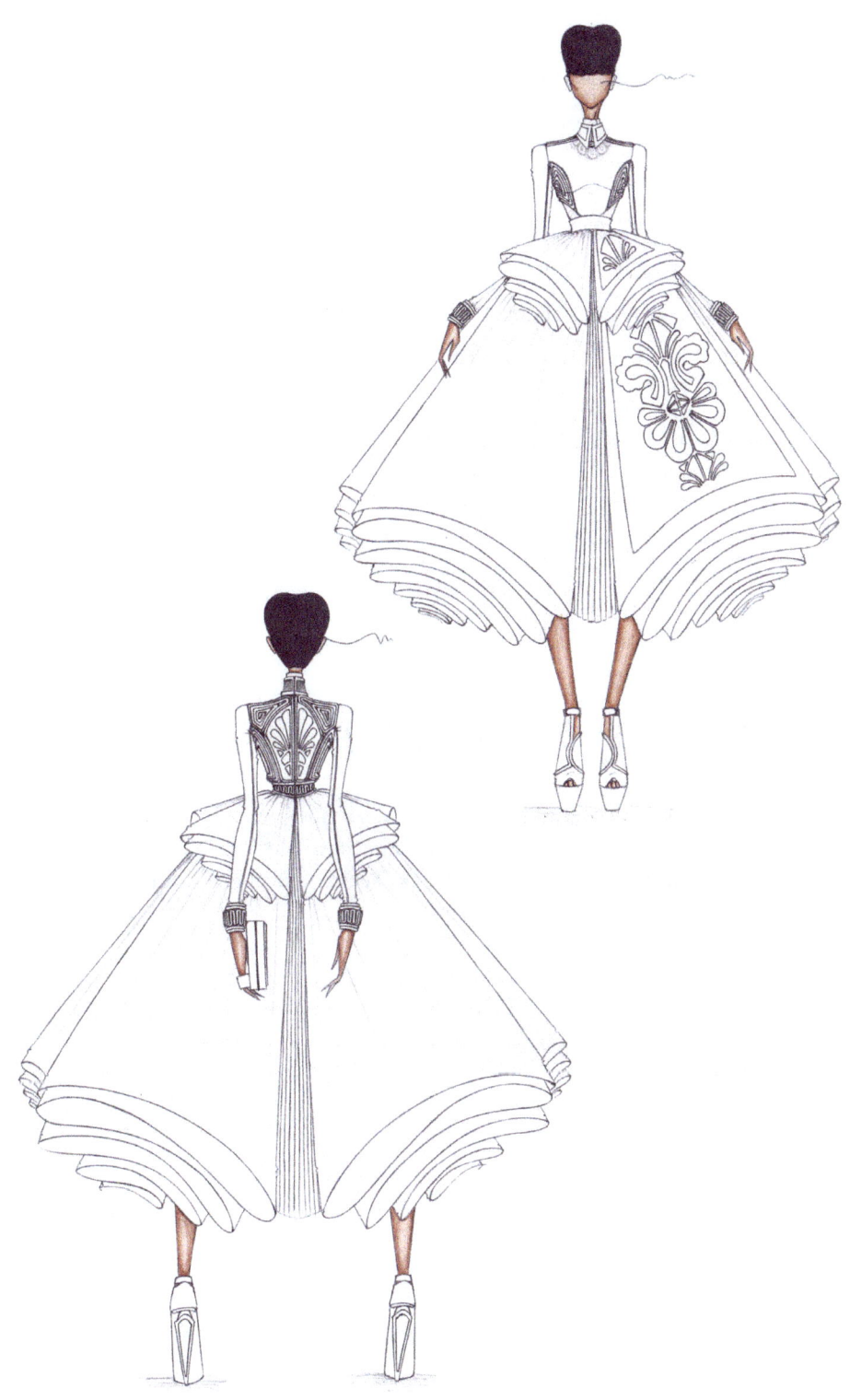

'I've always loved art in all forms ... I have a passion for fine art ... I can get lost in front of a painting, studying how the brushstrokes were used to convey a blushing cheek, the transparency of tulle or sheen of silk.'
Nelly Aba Mensah

NELLY ABA MENSAH

Fashion illustrator Nelly Aba Mensah recalls paging through her mother's vintage *Vogue* issues as a child and creating paper dolls for which she would draw hundreds of little paper outfits, cut them out, then glue them onto cardboard, oblivious to the fact that this could one day become a profession. Born in Russia, raised in Ghana, and now residing in San Francisco, Mensah's multi-cultural background pervades her work. For Mensah, fashion illustration is about more than just creating figures in the latest fashions; it has become a means to address and express her views on the lack of diversity in the fashion industry as a whole. Mensah utilizes traditional techniques over digital, drawing on the tactile nature of art supplies and how they stimulate all the senses, from chalk scratching paper, to the smell of gouache. Most of her illustrations are produced using mixed media, often combining graphite, pastels, watercolour, chalk and ink in the same illustration. Inspired by the subject at hand, Mensah's work at times captures carefree, uninhibited moments, her aesthetic moving from minimalist, with only a few lines, to opulent, richly patterned renderings bursting with colour.

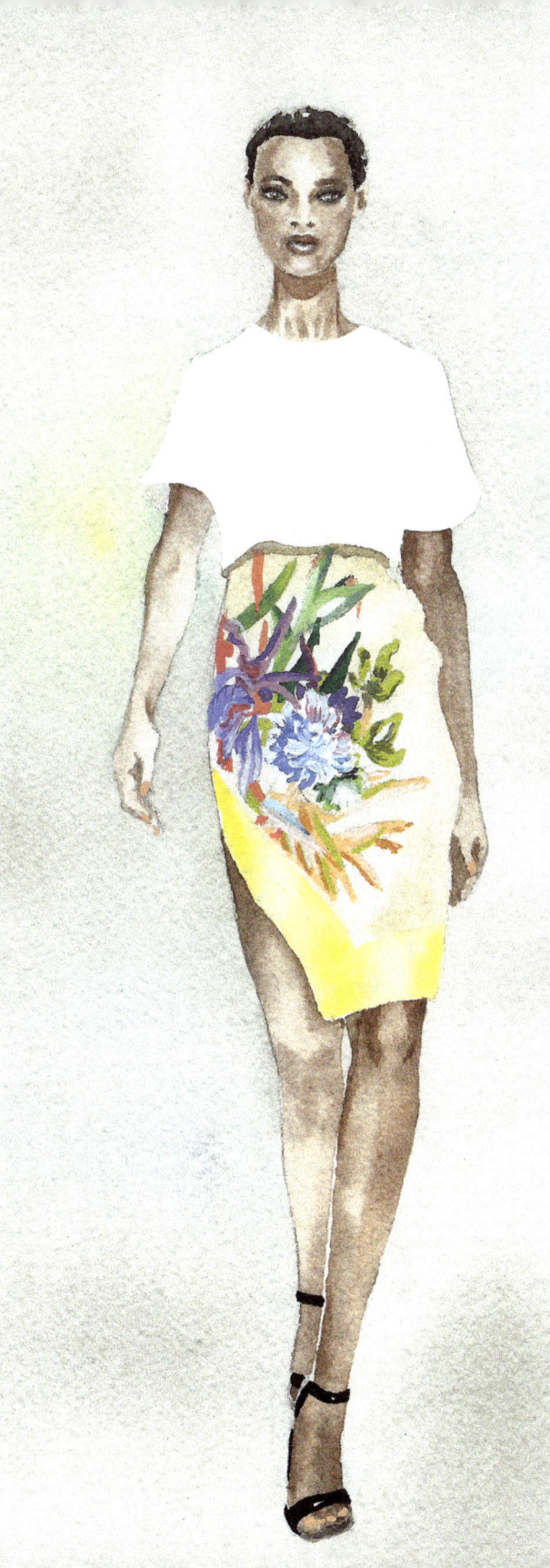

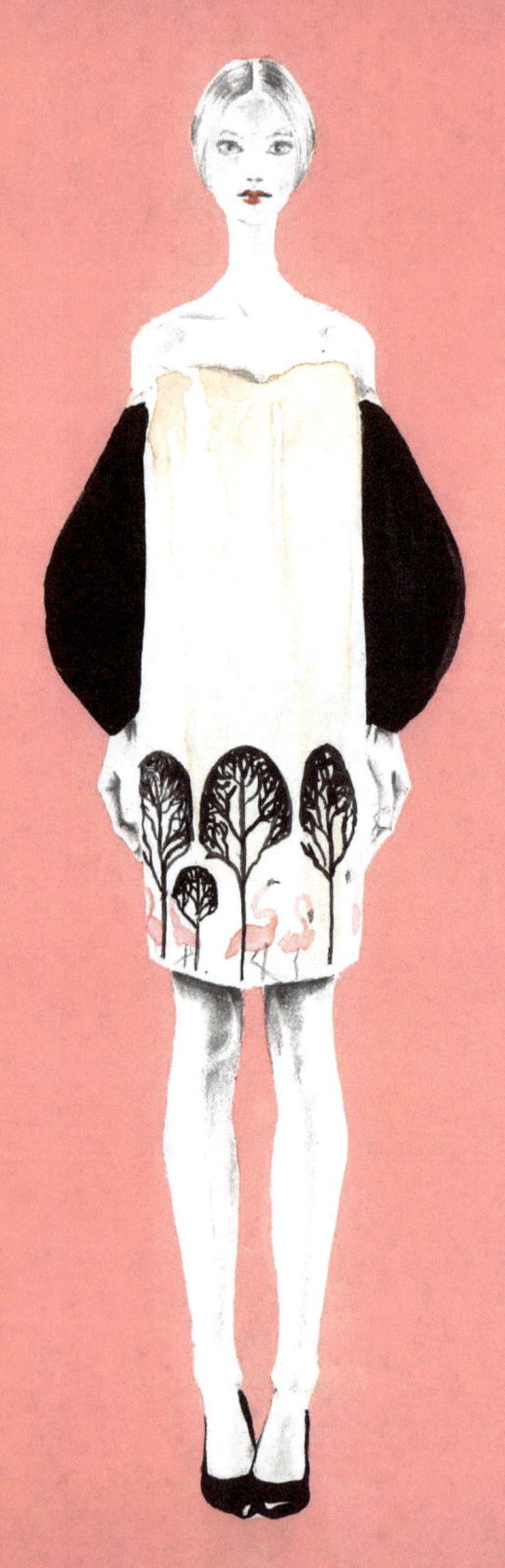

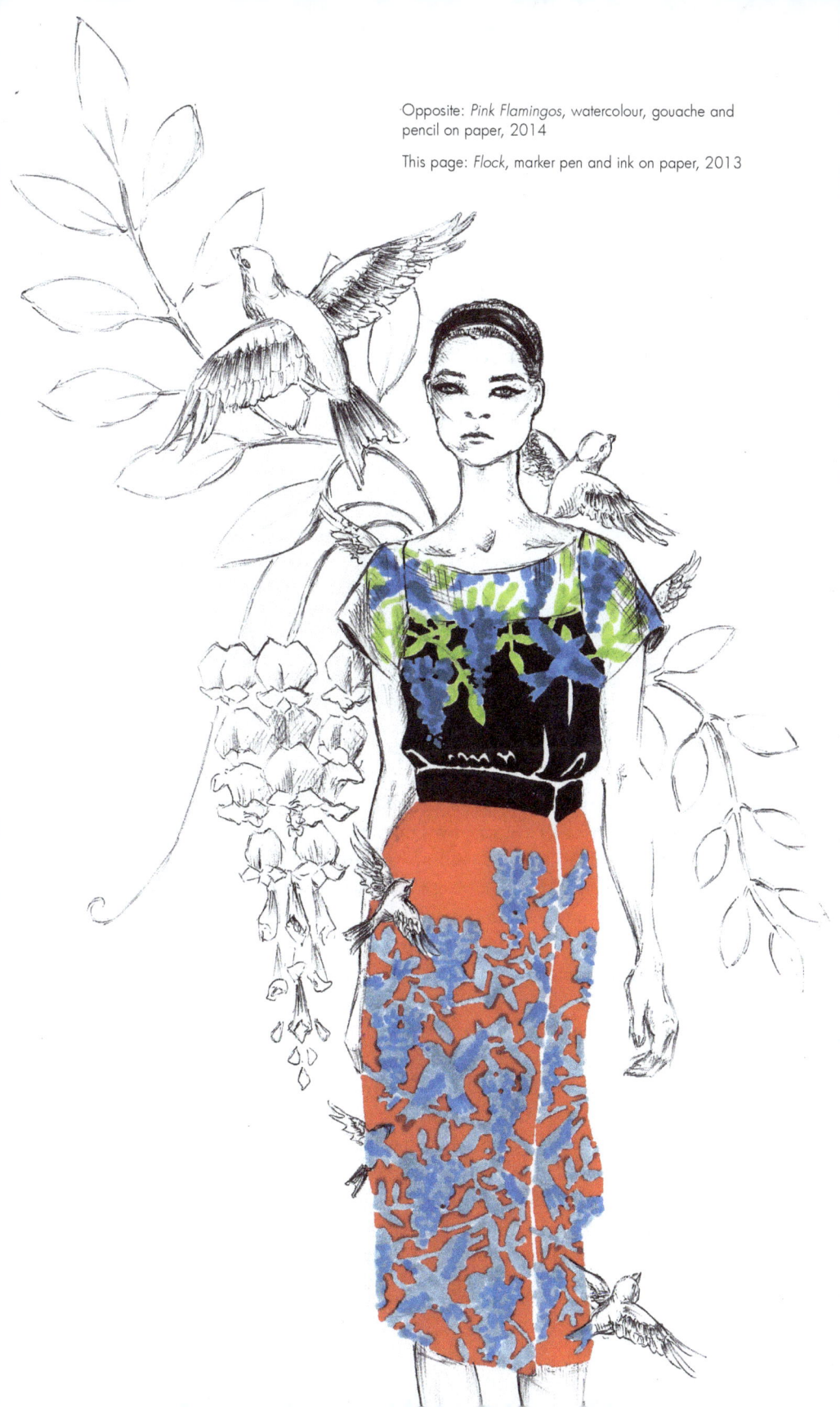

Opposite: *Pink Flamingos*, watercolour, gouache and pencil on paper, 2014

This page: *Flock*, marker pen and ink on paper, 2013

'My narrative art, which is a product
of my love for illustration, has
become my outlet for the type of
work I would like to see making
a comeback in the industry.'

Nicole Cronje

NICOLE CRONJE

Fashion illustration forms the basis of Nicole Cronje's artworks,
in which she creates rich narratives that draw the viewer into the
life of the heroines depicted within. For Cronje, every illustration
begins with imagining the subject's life, what she looks like, her
personality, her interests, right down to the subtle details such as
whether or not she would have freckles. The golden era of fashion
illustration is Cronje's major source of inspiration – one that, she
says, 'the crystalline photographs and computer-aided graphics of
today cannot hope to compete with.' This sentiment is what she
regards as the true purpose of the discipline: 'to inspire, summarize,
catalogue, and reflect not only the garments of an age but how it
feels to wear them.' Shunning computer work, which she describes
as 'torturous', Cronje favours hand-drawn techniques, embracing the
flaws such as pencil lines that are not completely erased to add depth.
Cronje's illustrations are feminine, quirky and light, resplendent
with pattern, colour, texture and reflective finishes, common
elements that result from working with pen, paint and metal-leaf.

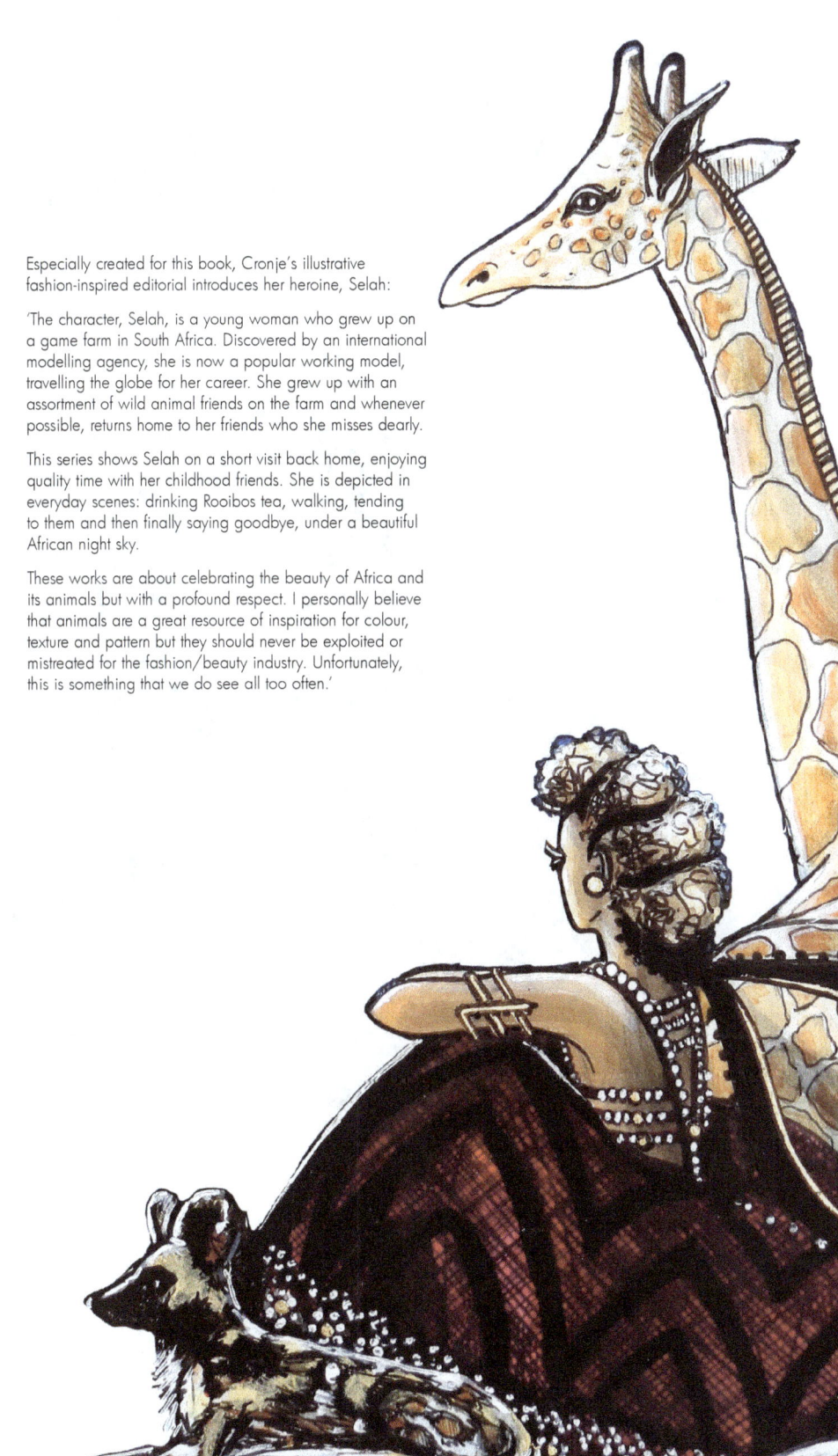

Especially created for this book, Cronje's illustrative fashion-inspired editorial introduces her heroine, Selah:

'The character, Selah, is a young woman who grew up on a game farm in South Africa. Discovered by an international modelling agency, she is now a popular working model, travelling the globe for her career. She grew up with an assortment of wild animal friends on the farm and whenever possible, returns home to her friends who she misses dearly.

This series shows Selah on a short visit back home, enjoying quality time with her childhood friends. She is depicted in everyday scenes: drinking Rooibos tea, walking, tending to them and then finally saying goodbye, under a beautiful African night sky.

These works are about celebrating the beauty of Africa and its animals but with a profound respect. I personally believe that animals are a great resource of inspiration for colour, texture and pattern but they should never be exploited or mistreated for the fashion/beauty industry. Unfortunately, this is something that we do see all too often.'

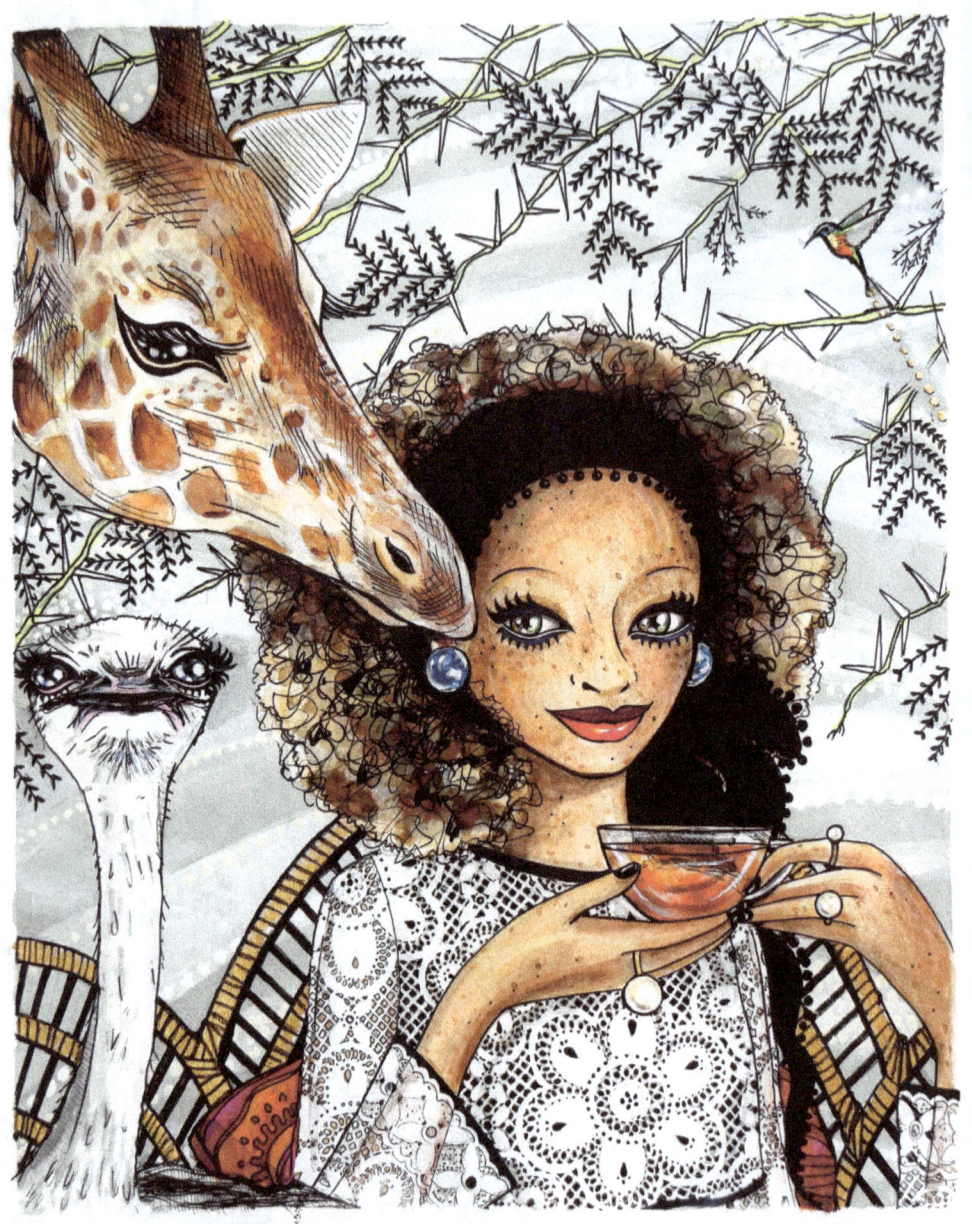

NICOLE CRONJE 2016

ROOIBOS TEA WITH FRIENDS

Rooibos Tea With Friends, mixed media on paper, 2016

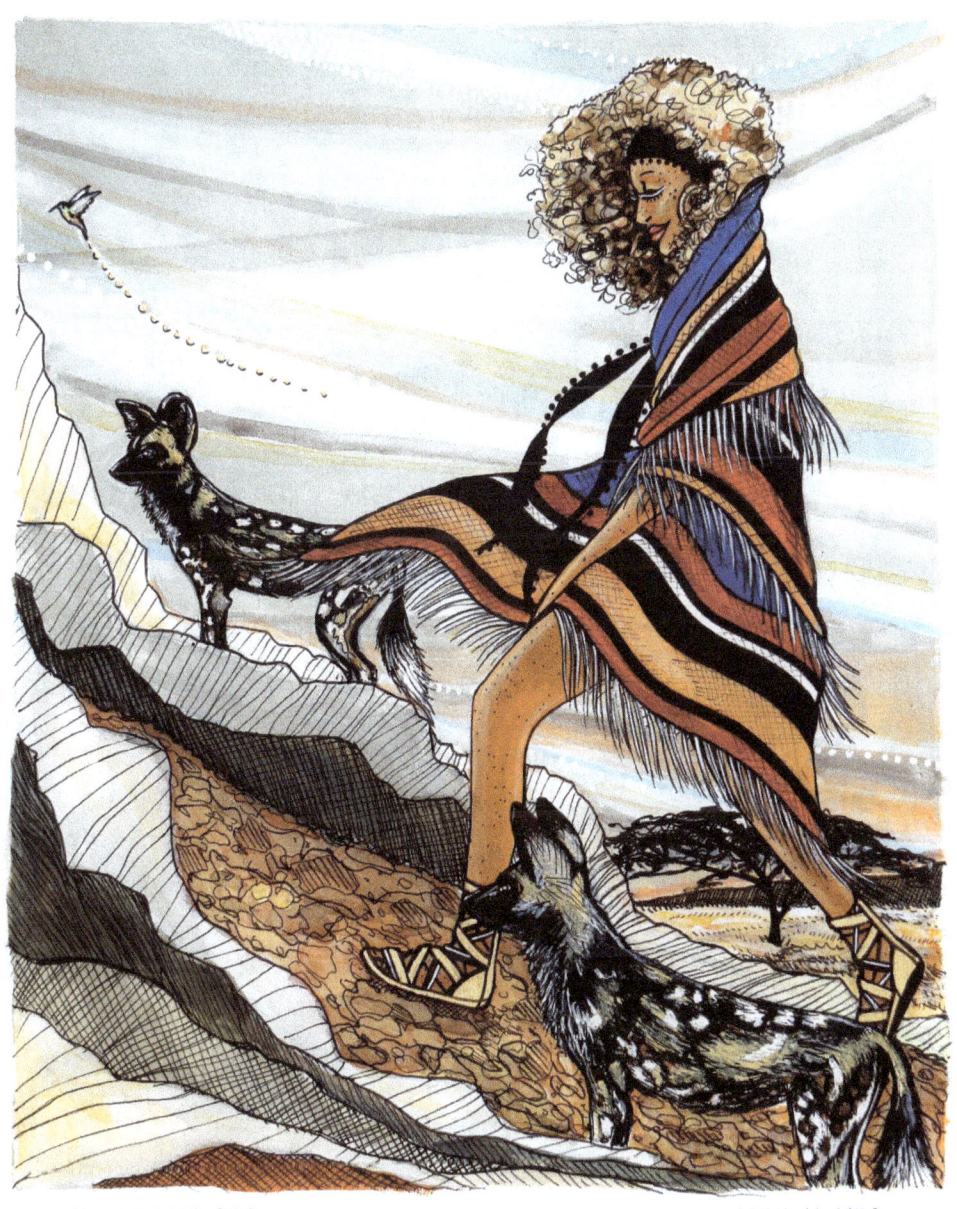

NICOLE CRONJE 2016   WALKING WILD

Walking Wild, mixed media on paper, 2016

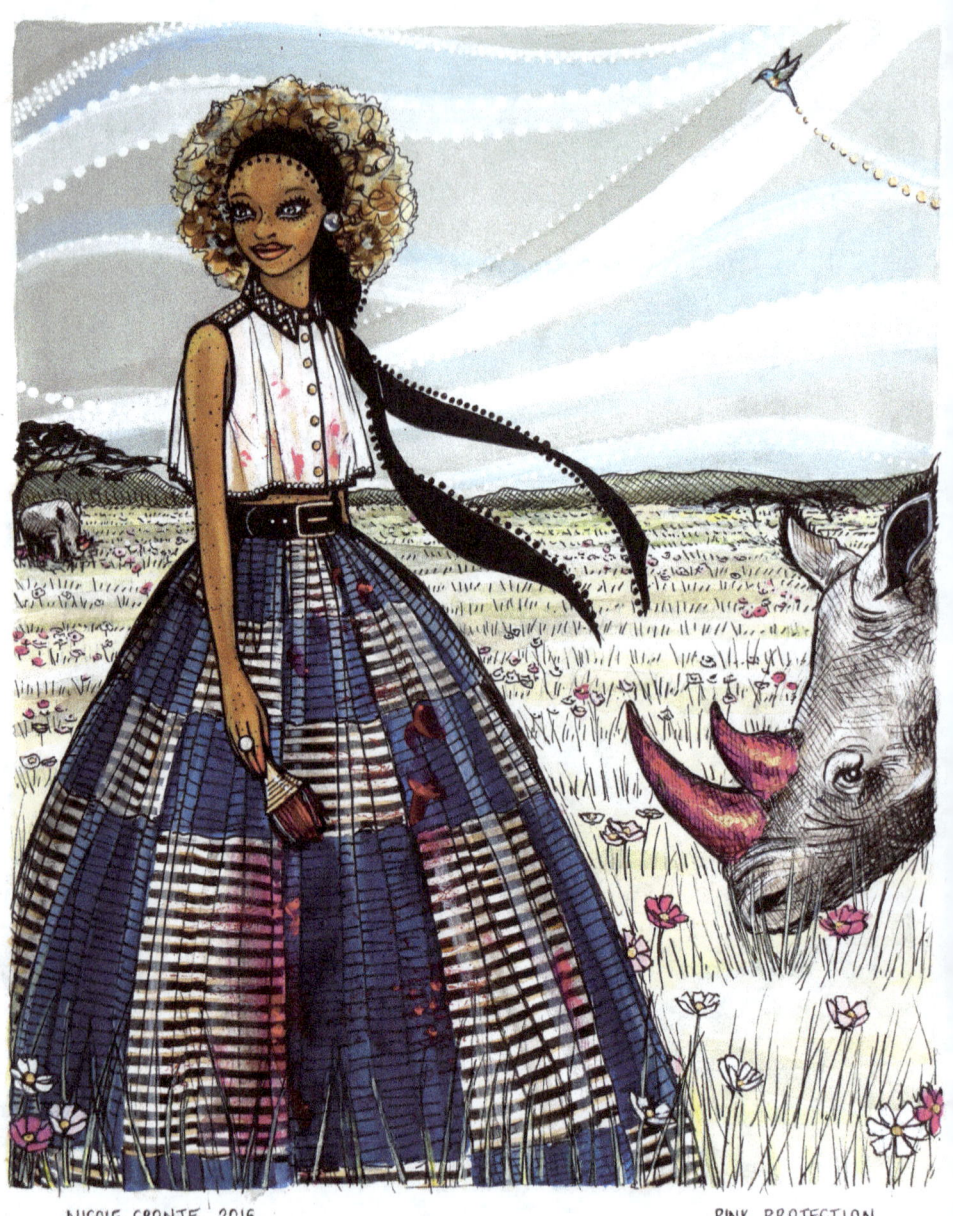

NICOLE CRONJE 2016

PINK PROTECTION

Pink Protection, mixed media on paper, 2016

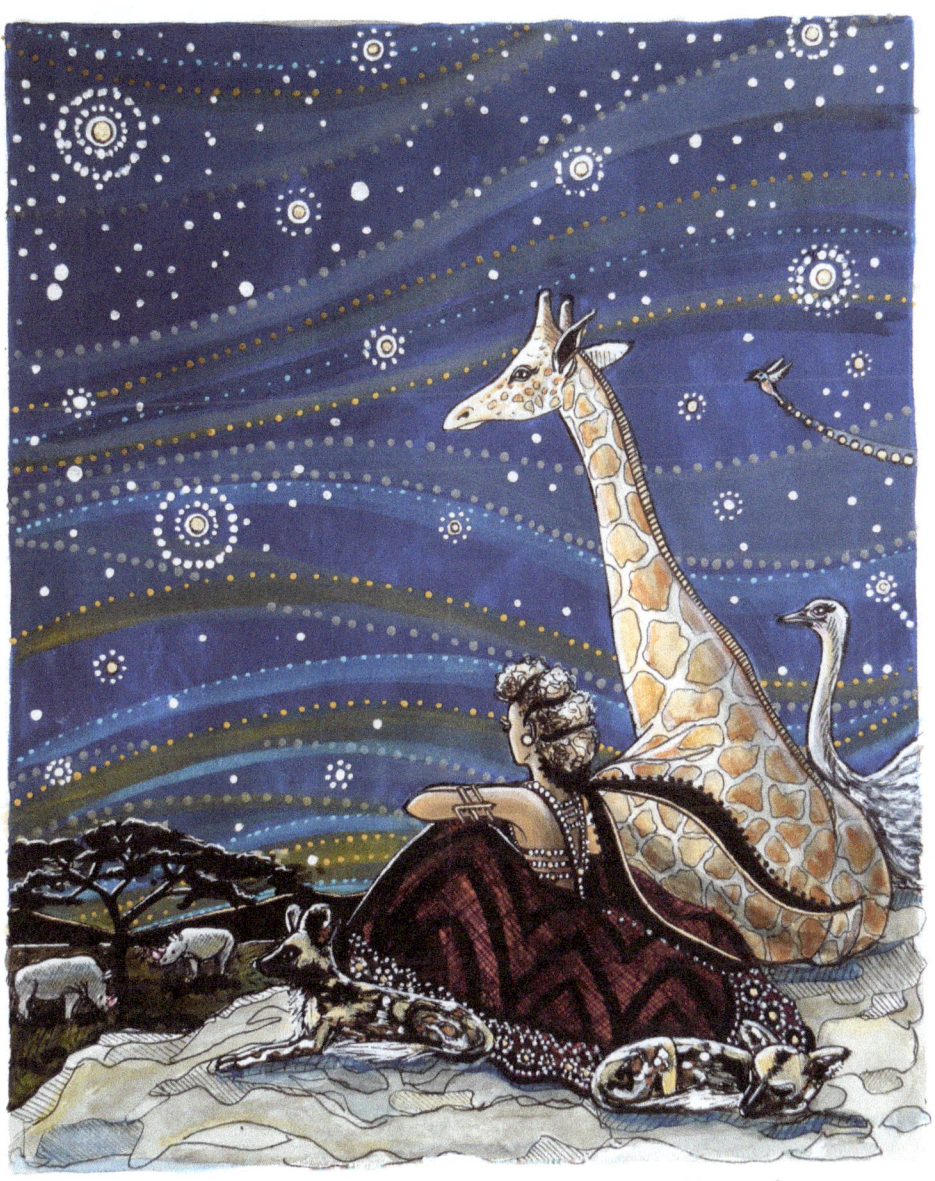

NICOLE CRONJE 2016   GO WELL , STAY WELL

Go Well, Stay Well, mixed media on paper, 2016

'My favourite form of medium is everything. There is just something about mixed media that just gives life to an illustration ... it allows the viewer to interact with your illustrations more.'

Nyorh Agwe

NYORH AGWE

Fashion designer and illustrator Nyorh Agwe's aesthetic is a layering of traditional techniques with new technology, and is significantly marked by culture. A graduate of Parsons School of Design, Agwe draws heavily on the fearless, creative energy of New York City where she lives and works. Agwe also incorporates her Cameroonian heritage in the form of the big, bold, colourful, and dramatic style of traditional Cameroonian dress, evident in her tall, straight figures enveloped in voluminous silhouettes. As she says, 'The bigger the clothes the more room I have to play with. The more movement I can portray.' Fully embracing the possibilities of multi-media, Agwe's illustrations combine digital graphics, collage, illustration, and photography in a continuous process of seamlessly switching between hand-drawn and digital, stating that, 'I find mixing hand techniques with digital techniques adds dimension to my drawings and just makes the process all the more enjoyable and boundless.' This continuous experimentation gives Agwe's illustrations a distinctive futuristic edge.

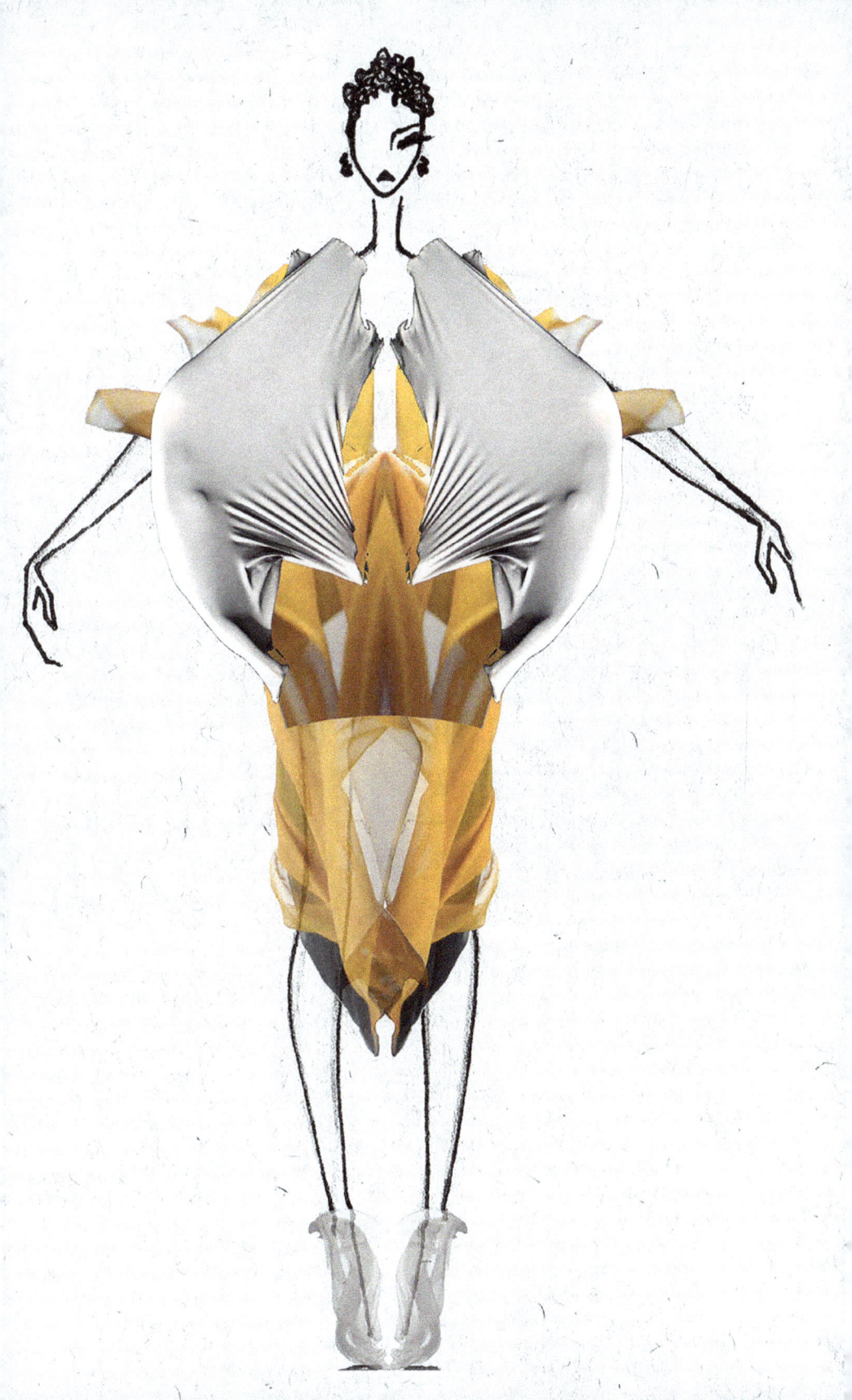

Tamed Freedom, mixed media (Photoshop, Illustrator, photographs of fabric draping in chiffon, jersey and organza, and pen on canvas paper), 2014

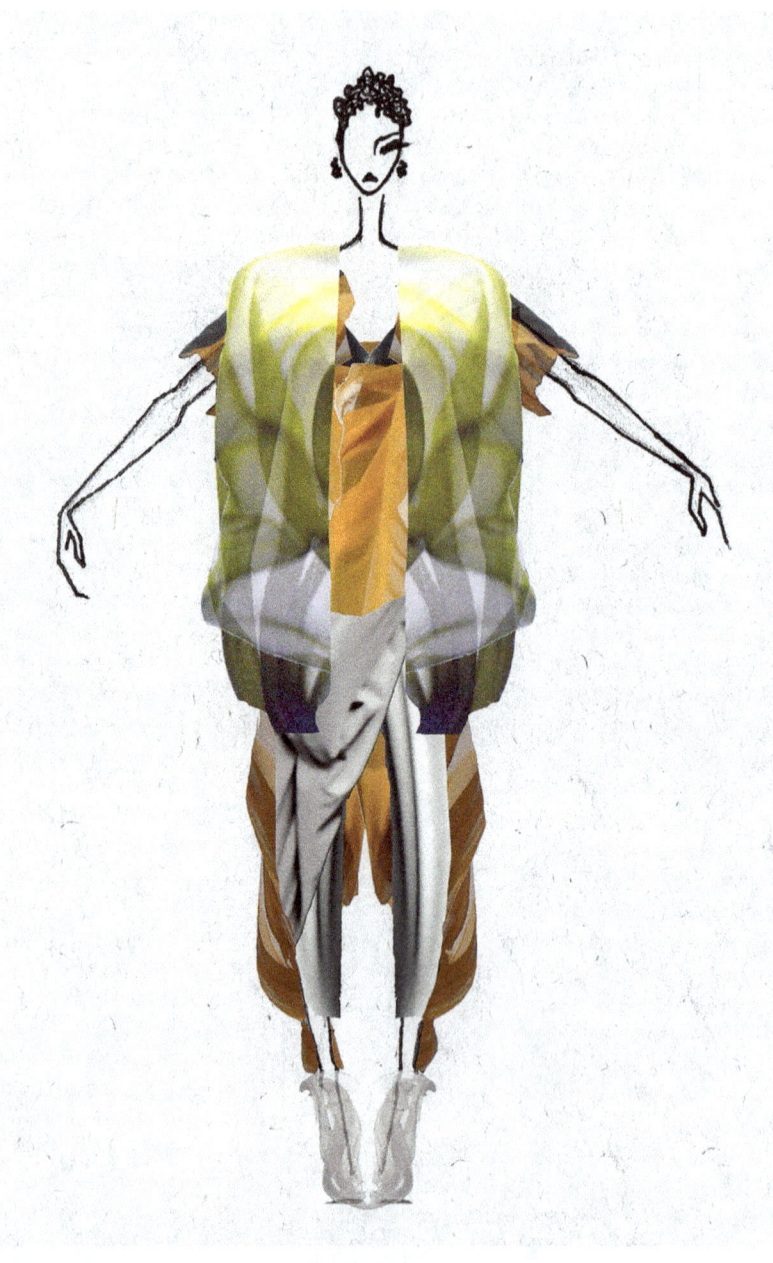

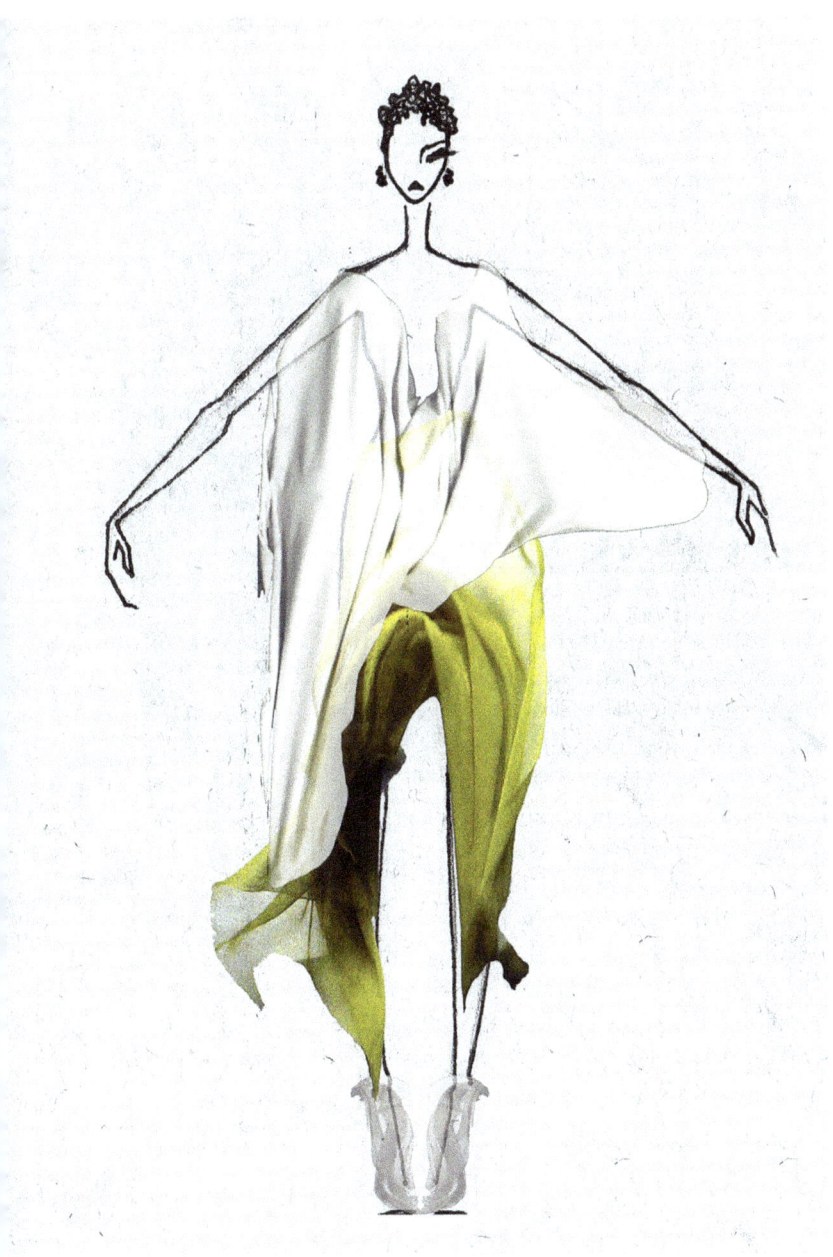

Denola Grey, digital illustration using Procreate, 2015

'I didn't get into fashion illustration by accident. I have always loved drawing ... I fell in love with it and I haven't looked back since.'

Okhai 'Lean Kid'

OKHAI 'LEAN KID'

Nigerian fashion illustrator Okhai has always been passionate about drawing. He began creating illustrations for t-shirts whilst still in secondary school, and was later encouraged by a fashion designer friend to try his hand at illustrating clothing. Okhai draws his inspiration from people, observation, fabric and music. His illustrations start off as pencil sketches on paper and are then scanned and brushed up digitally, the medium he prefers due to the ease with which he is able to adjust mistakes, as well as the ability to play around with ideas. Okhai is one of the few illustrators featured in this book who turns his attention toward illustrating male figures, including a series dedicated to capturing the style of his country's dapper trendsetters. He also collaborates with local fashion designers, and has been called upon to document Lagos Fashion Week collections.

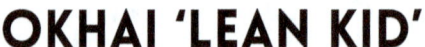

Right: *Denola Grey*, digital illustration using Procreate, 2016

Below: *Nobs*, digital illustration using Procreate, 2015

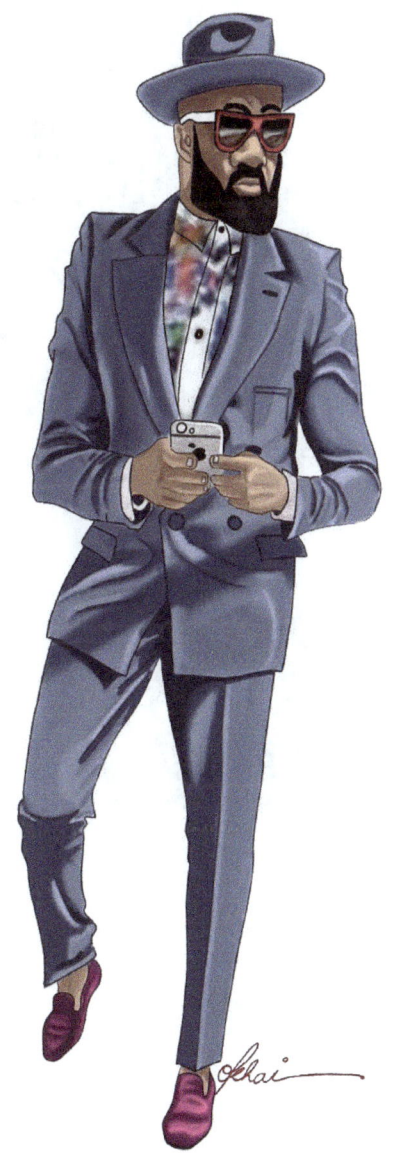

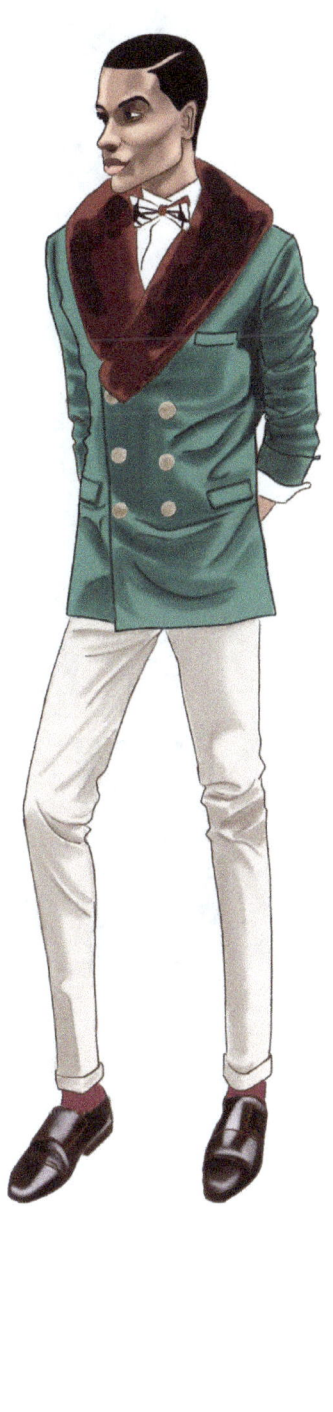

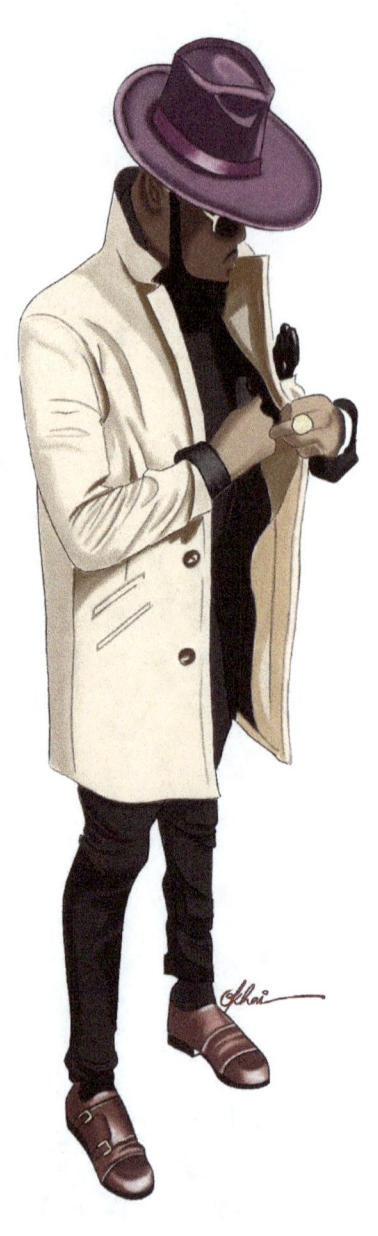
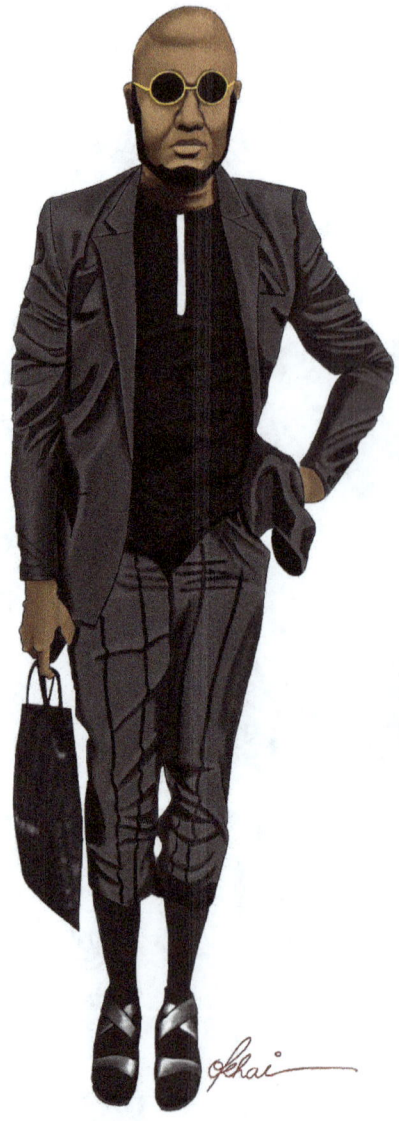

Left: *Ayo*, digital illustration using Procreate, 2016

Right: *The Style Infidel*, digital illustration using Procreate, 2015

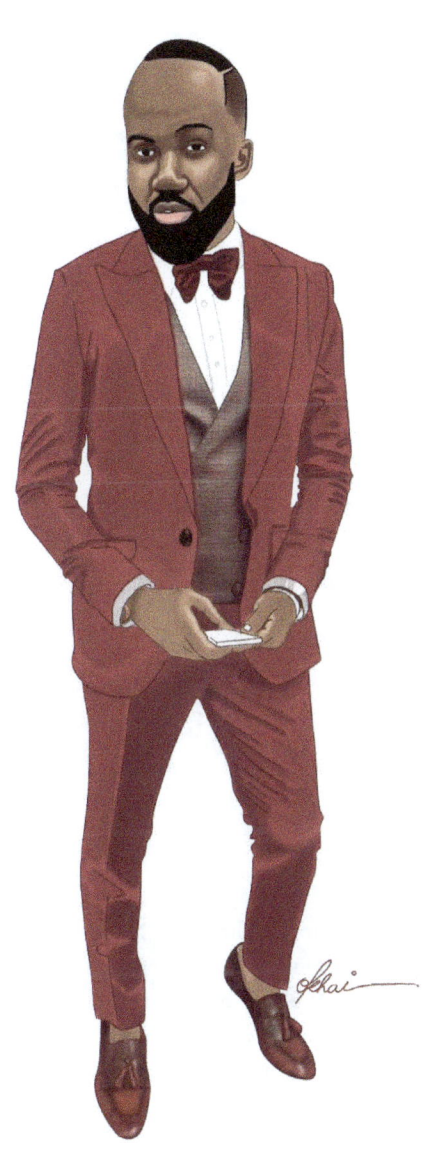
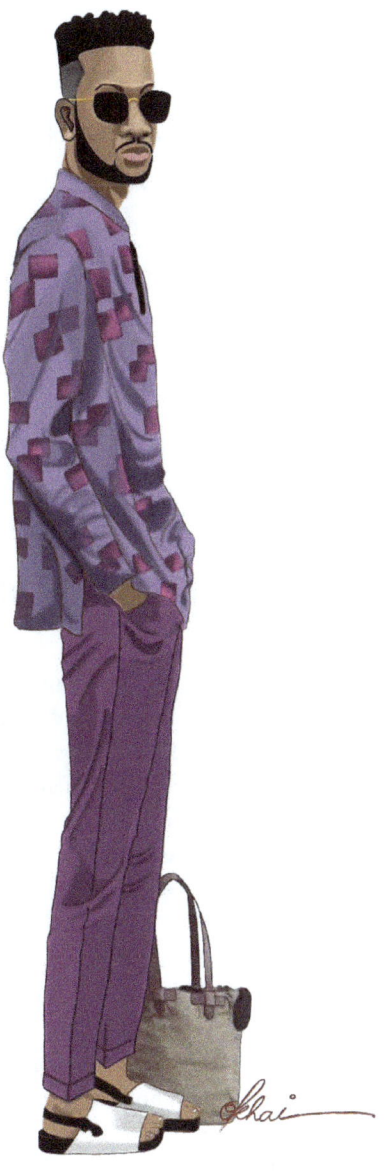

Left: *Noble Igwe*, digital illustration using Procreate, 2015

Right: *Orange Culture*, digital illustration using Procreate, 2015

'I try to change the existing mental
visuals of the African woman
to the foreigner. I do this by
sketching very powerful-looking
women in powerful clothing.'

Papa Oppong

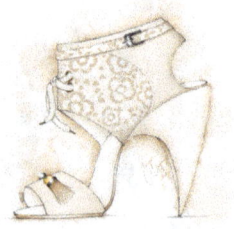

PAPA OPPONG

Papa Oppong began fashion illustration as a hobby, a way to pass time.
He later went on to study fashion design at Radford University College
in Ghana. Focusing on womenswear, Oppong's illustrations depict strong,
powerful-looking women rendered in his signature style of bright colours
and the whimsically exaggerated silhouettes that belie a more serious message.
Portraying imagined and existing personalities, Oppong uses his work to
challenge existing mental visuals of African women in a global world, stating
that he wants his illustrations to depict 'African women who are strong,
modern, romantic, and very much in control of their sexuality.' Another
characteristic flowing through most of his illustrations is his signature floral
print called 'Poison Bush', formed of bold, messy strokes of colour when
viewed up close, transforming into pretty blossoms when viewed from afar.
Oppong uses both traditional hand-drawn and modern digital methods of
illustration, citing the latter as his personal preference due to the greater control
it provides in achieving cleaner, mistake-free results, and more importantly
the fact that he cannot run out of colour, making it a cost effective option.
Oppong does, however, utilize traditional methods, drawing with marker
pen and inks when looking to create artwork with a more personal touch.

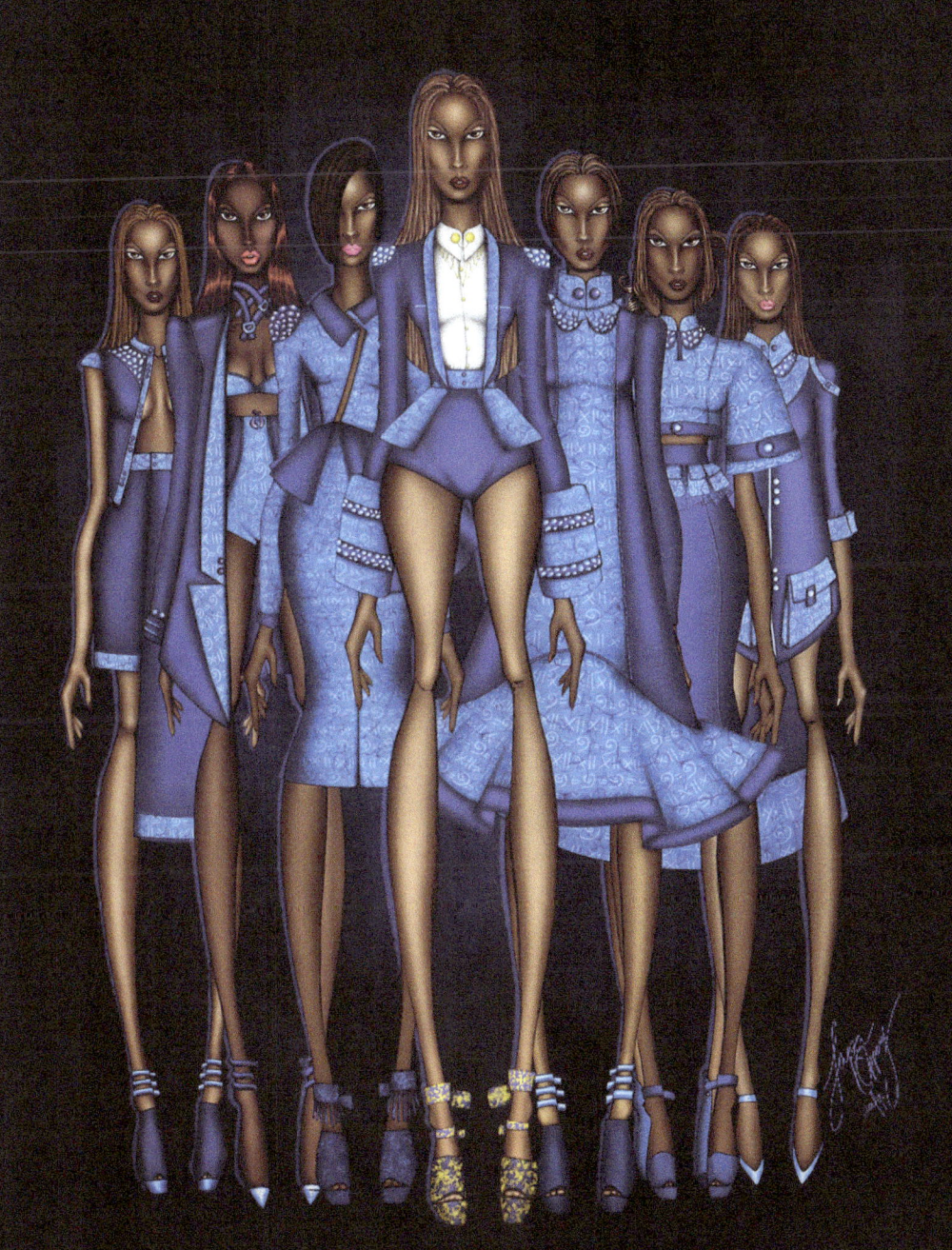

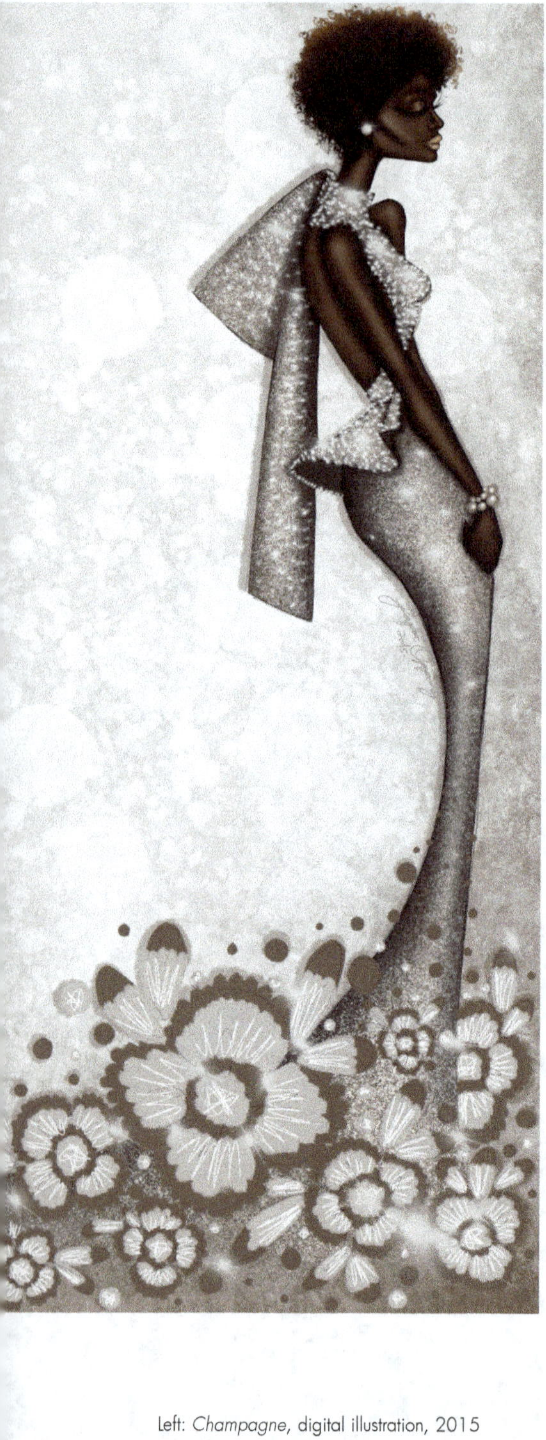

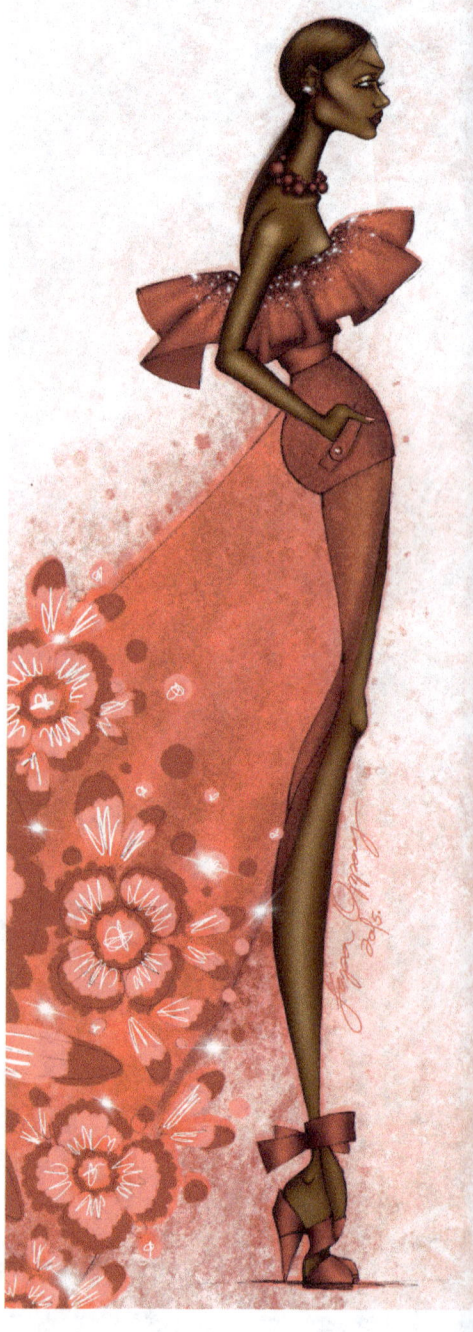

Left: *Champagne*, digital illustration, 2015

Right: *Scarlet*, digital illustration, 2015

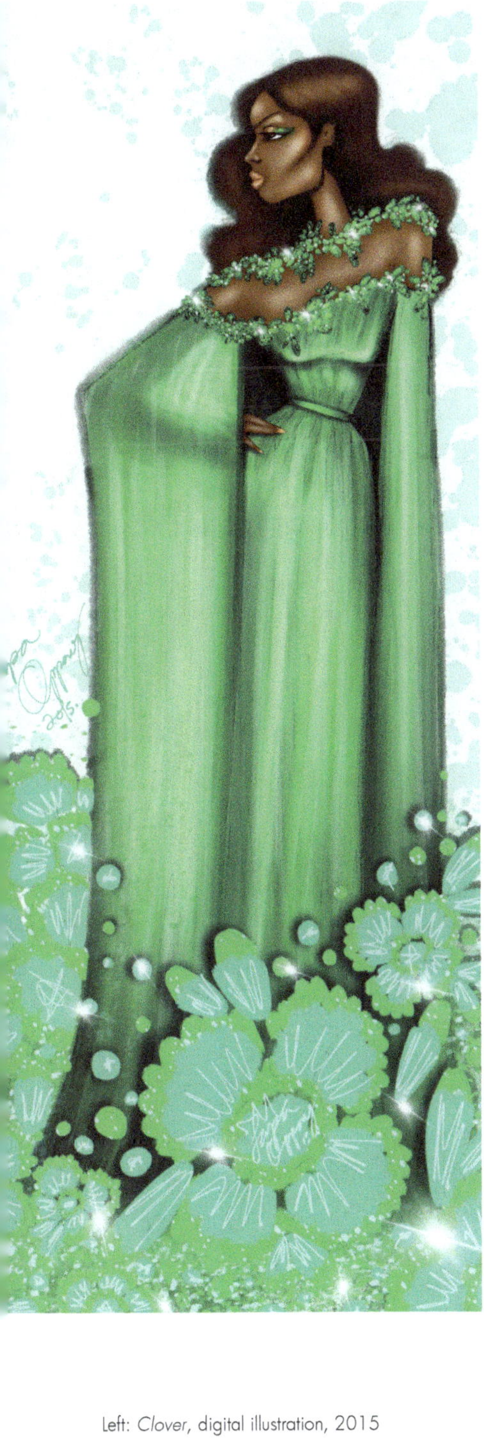

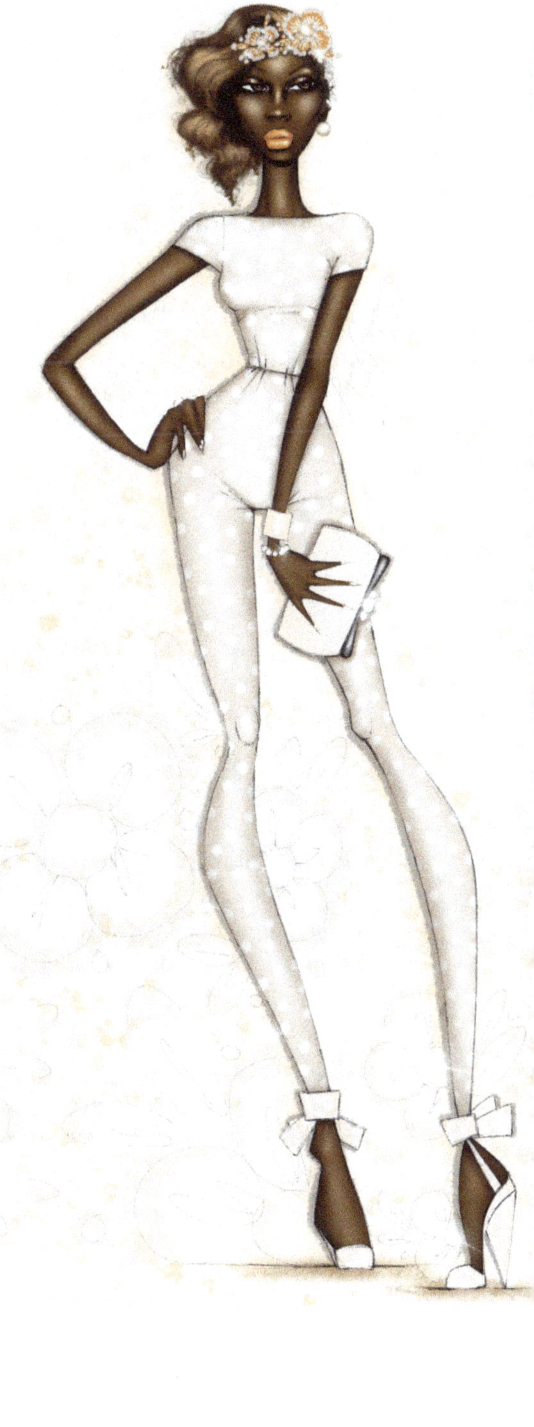

Left: *Clover*, digital illustration, 2015

Right: *Polka*, digital illustration, 2015

'Fashion illustration is
never something I dreamt
of as a career path.'

Peniel Enchill

PENIEL ENCHILL

Peniel Enchill is a UK-based fashion illustrator of Ghanaian
heritage. She came to the discipline after wanting to become a
fashion designer and having a proclivity for spending her days
drawing anything fashion related. Enchill started out working
with acrylics, but has since moved into digital illustration, which
has seen her lean towards a photorealism-inspired aesthetic.
Enchill's illustrations are not solely focused on portraying the
clothing and adornment aspect of fashion. She often employs
a narrative-style setting depicting beautiful, sophisticated,
successful, life-loving, everyday women of colour, images rarely
given prominence in mainstream global media outlets.

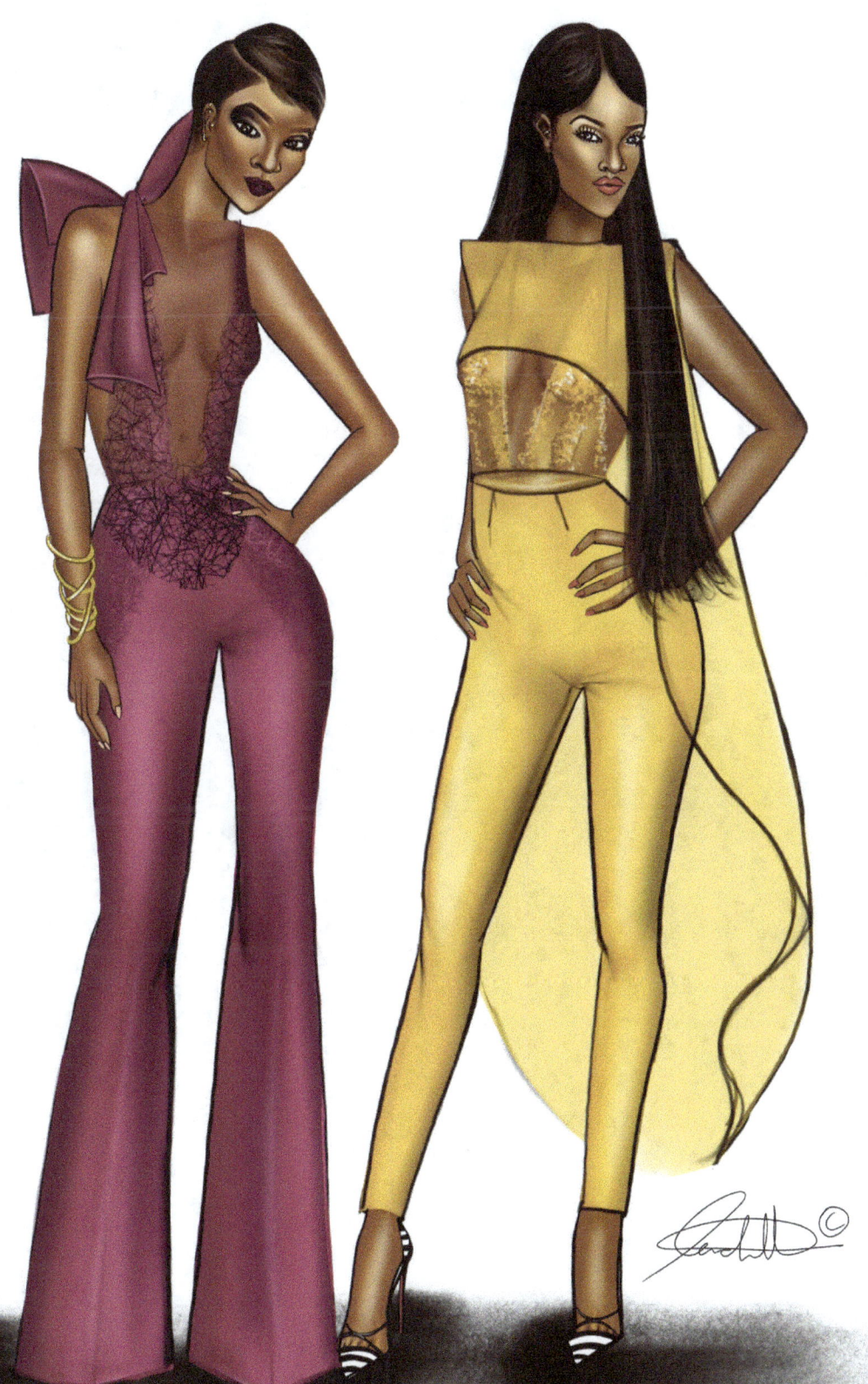

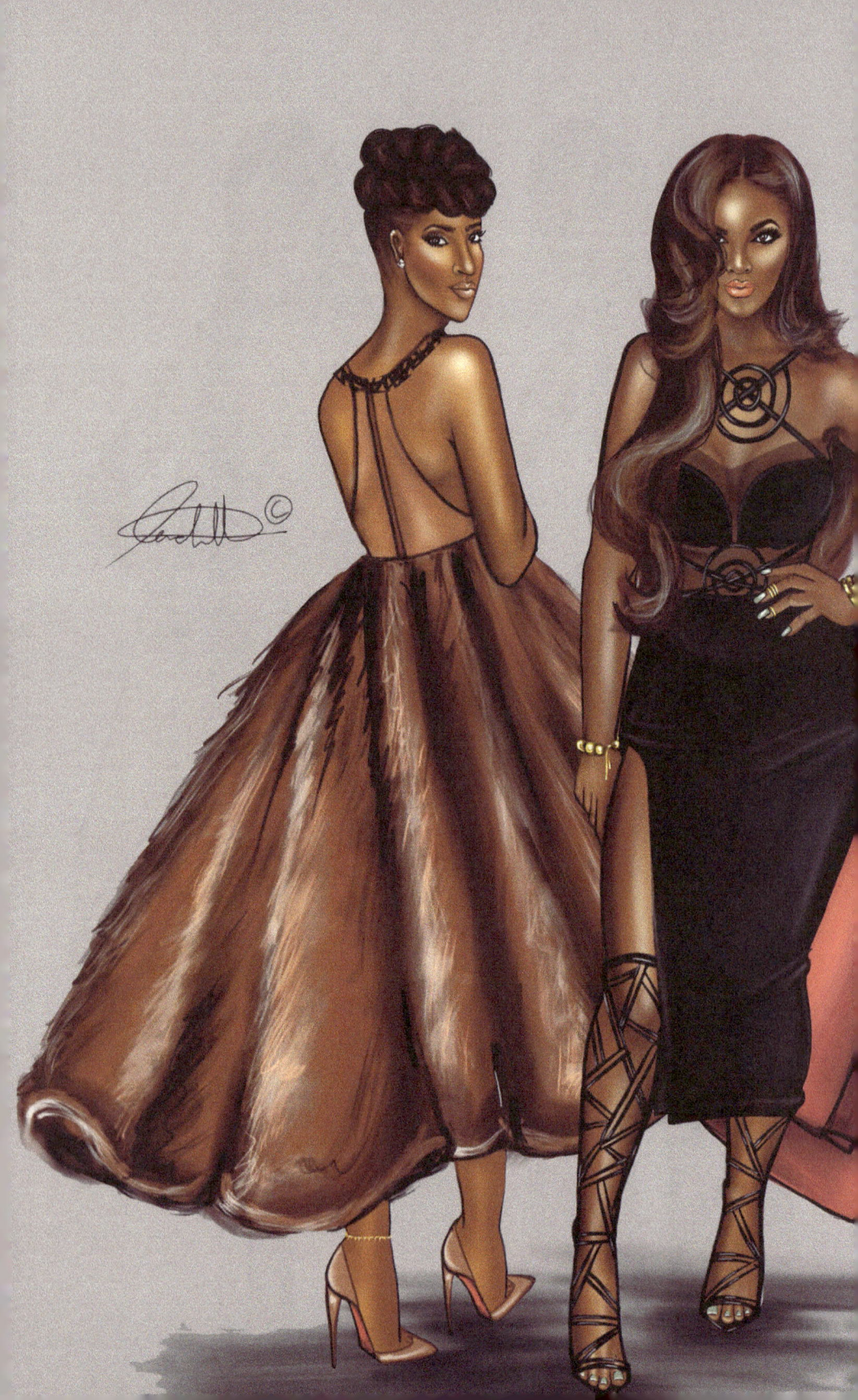

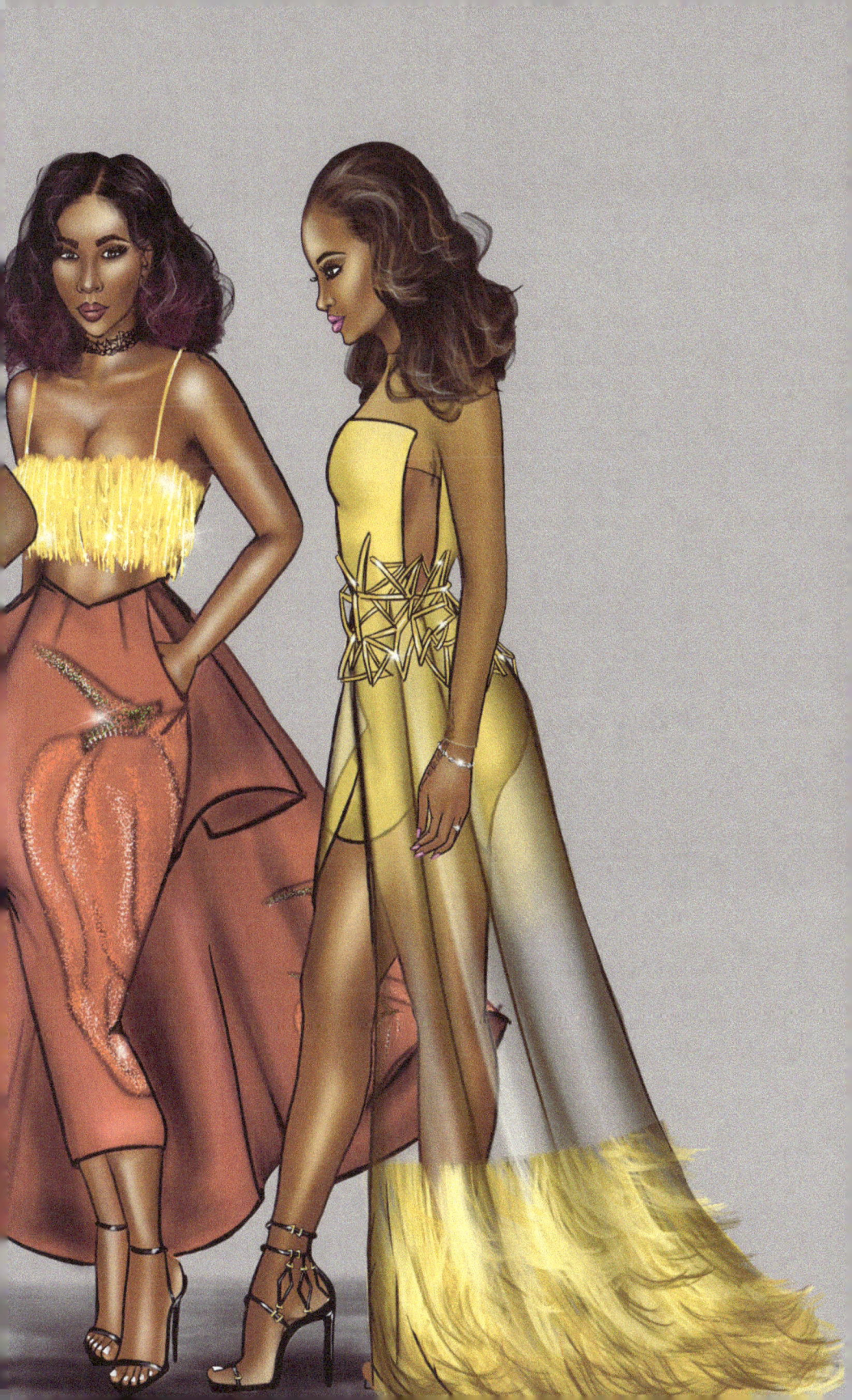

'I love the idea of creating an identity so unique that people would be able to recognize that it's yours without being told so.'

Pola Maneli

POLA MANELI

Pola Maneli is a freelance illustrator and art director whose work is a social commentary on 'blackness', touching on themes including identity, popular culture and politics. Born and raised in Port Elizabeth, South Africa, the influence of traditional culture is also evident in Maneli's work, showing up in his signature style of razor sharp triangular lines, simplified forms which are based on Ndebele patterns. Most of his work is digitally rendered, based on pencil studies and compositions. Maneli cites photography and fashion as key sources of inspiration, and these are regularly referenced in his work. An interest in comics drew Maneli's attention to the high level of care and detail employed by Japanese anime creators in creating their characters' clothing. This fueled an obsession with dressing his own characters in garments that transcend a utilitarian function, exhibiting instead a broader concept or tone. Although not a 'fashion illustrator' in the traditional sense, Maneli's 'Street Wear' series – a conceptual collection of fashion illustrations in the form of a look book – was a way to explore and show his appreciation for fashion. Fashion is a discipline he views as 'just another, medium – albeit a singularly unique one – to express [his] voice through.'

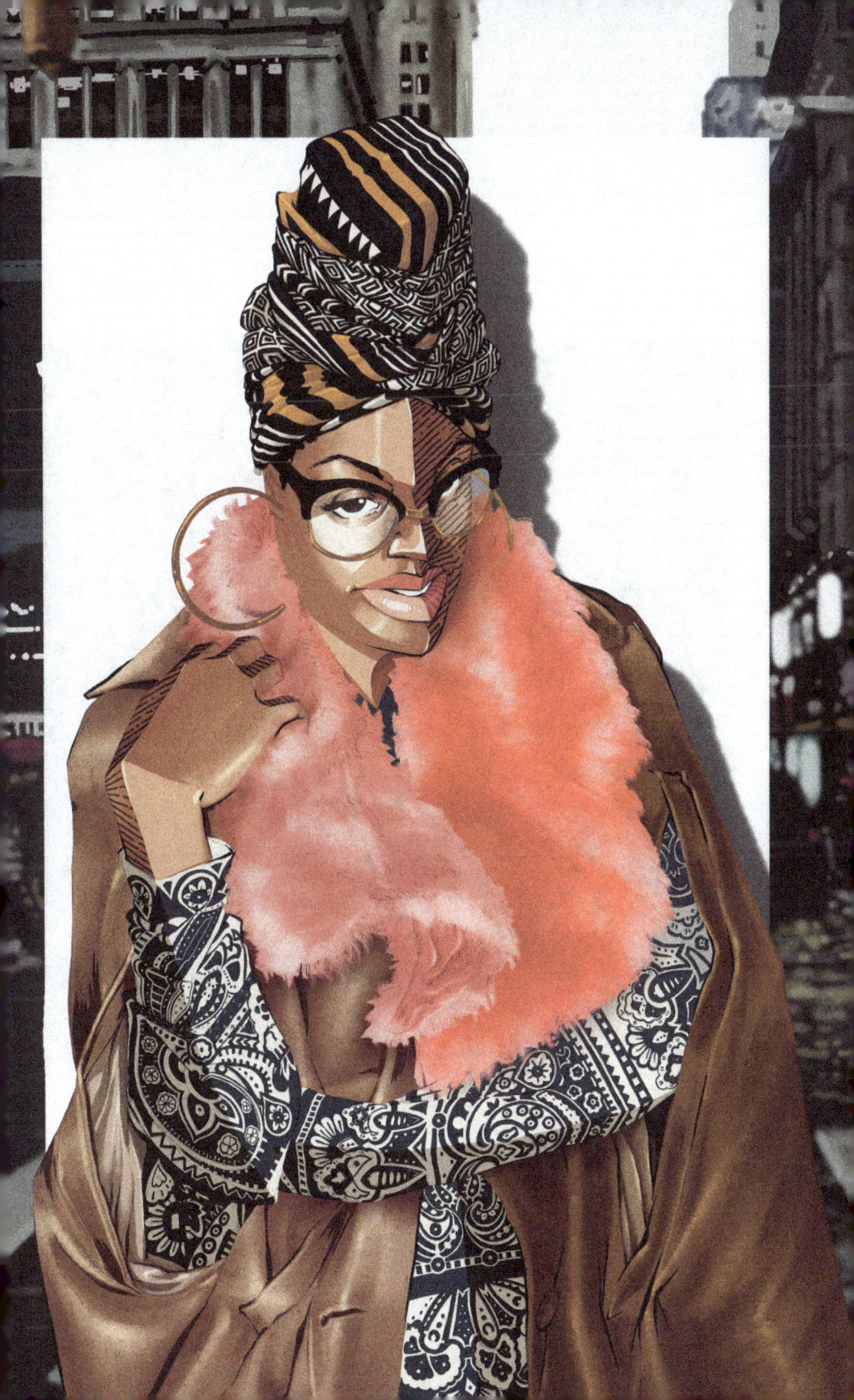

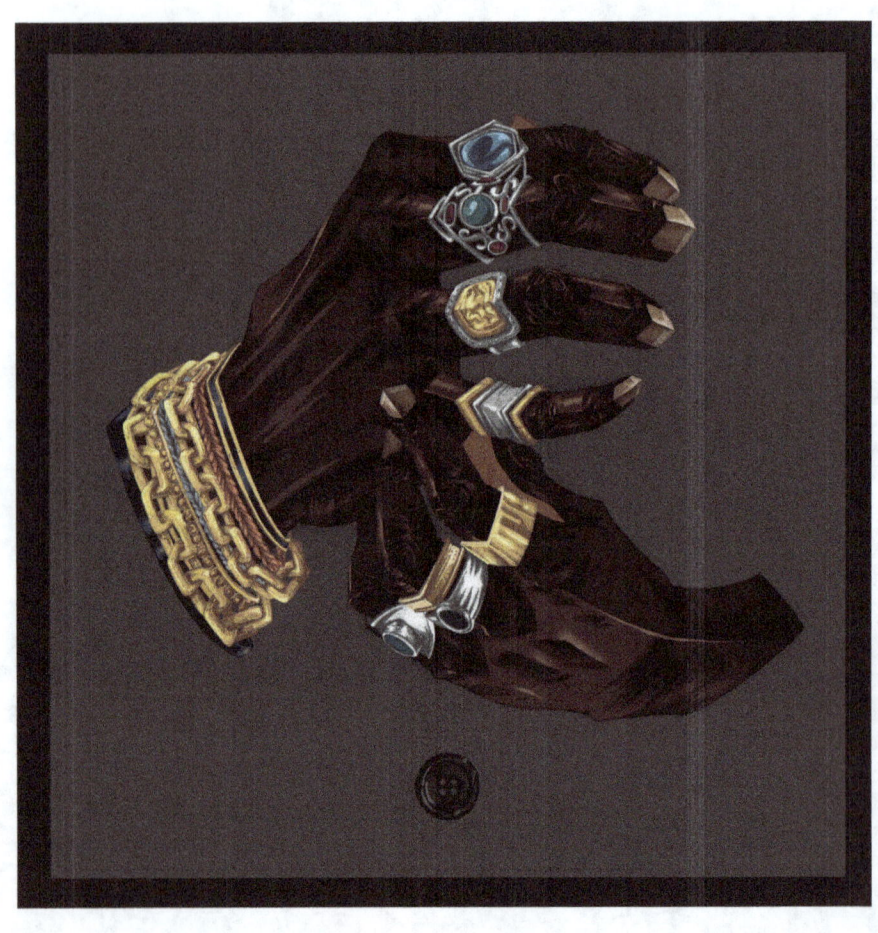

This page: *Slumflower 4*, graphite and Photoshop, 2015

Opposite: *Beanie Boy*, graphite and Photoshop, 2015

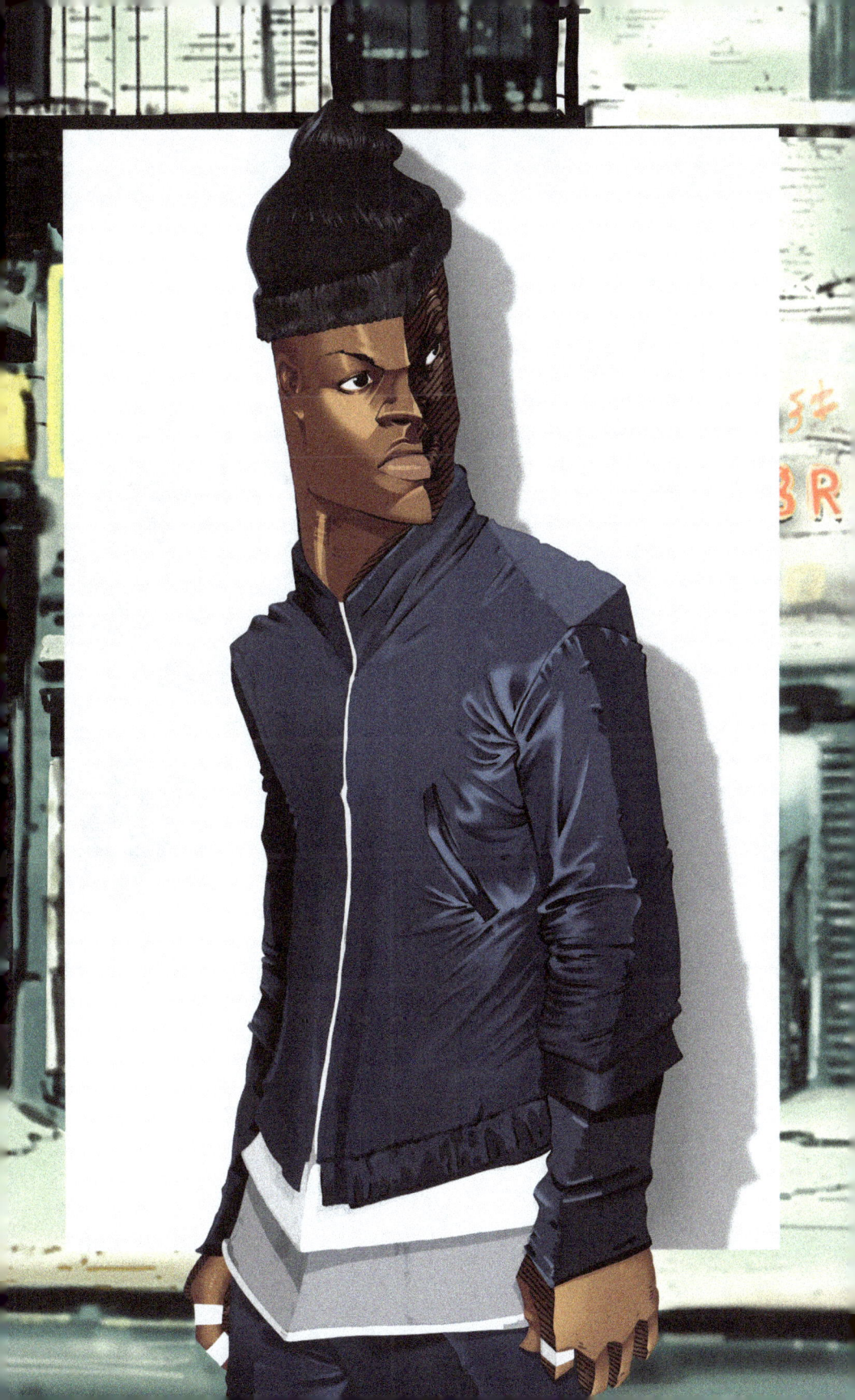

'[Illustration] is part of my work process … It is my favourite way of explaining the ideas behind my designs … I can't feel like I've finished my work if I didn't create illustrations.'

Sonia Merabet

SONIA MERABET

Sonia Merabet is an Algerian fashion designer. She studied in the UK, and lives and works in Algiers. Illustration is a significant part of Merabet's fashion design process, which she sees as an easy way to express the ideas behind her designs. Shaped by her research and ideas, Merabet's illustrative style is a complementary response to the theme of each collection. She prefers to sketch quite quickly, so mainly works with pen, coloured pens and crayons as they enable her to do so. Merabet, however, is not afraid to experiment with other mediums, working with anything that will enable her to achieve what she requires visually. This has seen her incorporate collages, photography and fabric – and as an example of embracing what she has on hand, for her Malcolm X-inspired collection, Merabet experimented with black pen and corrector fluid on brown Kraft paper.

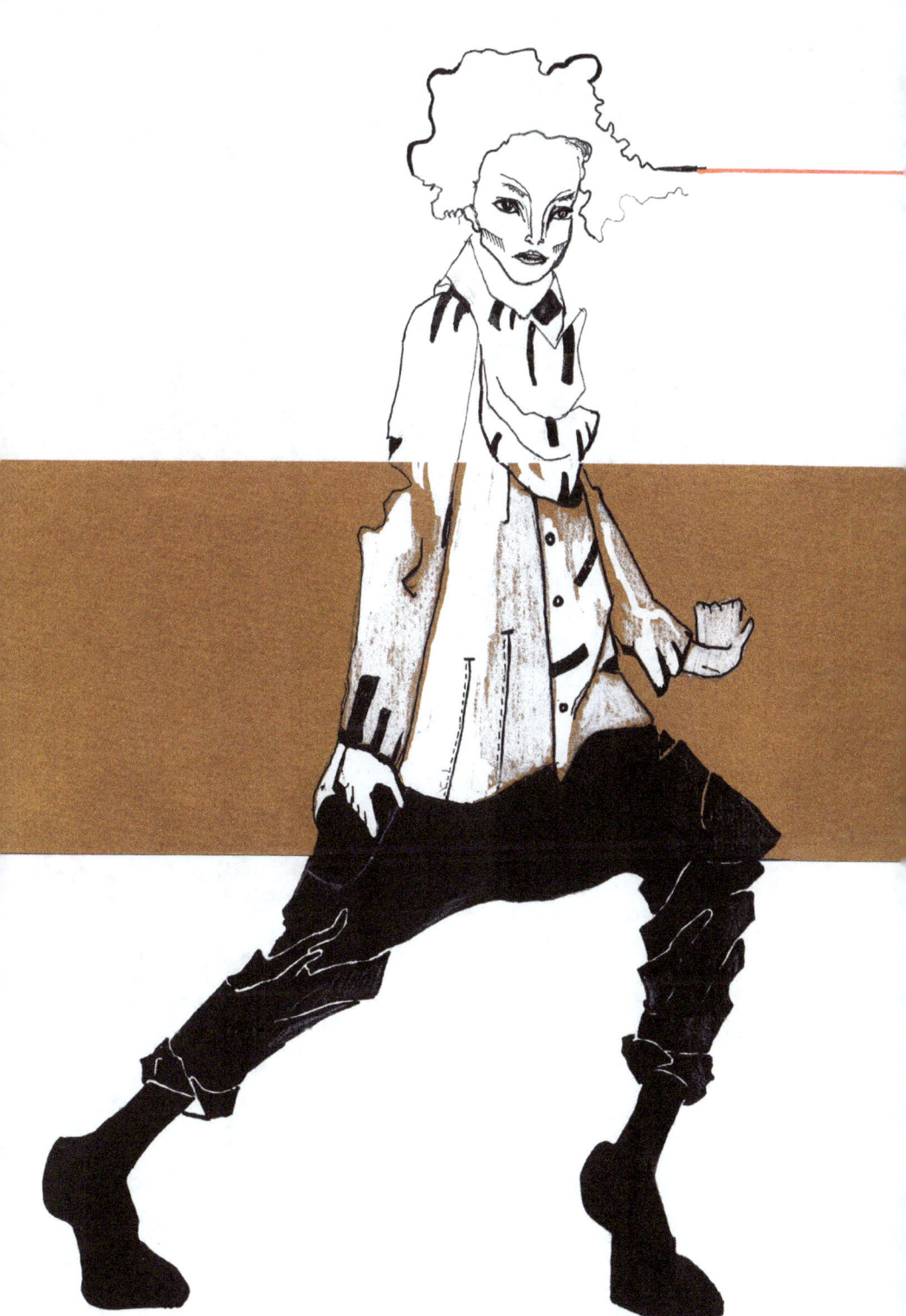

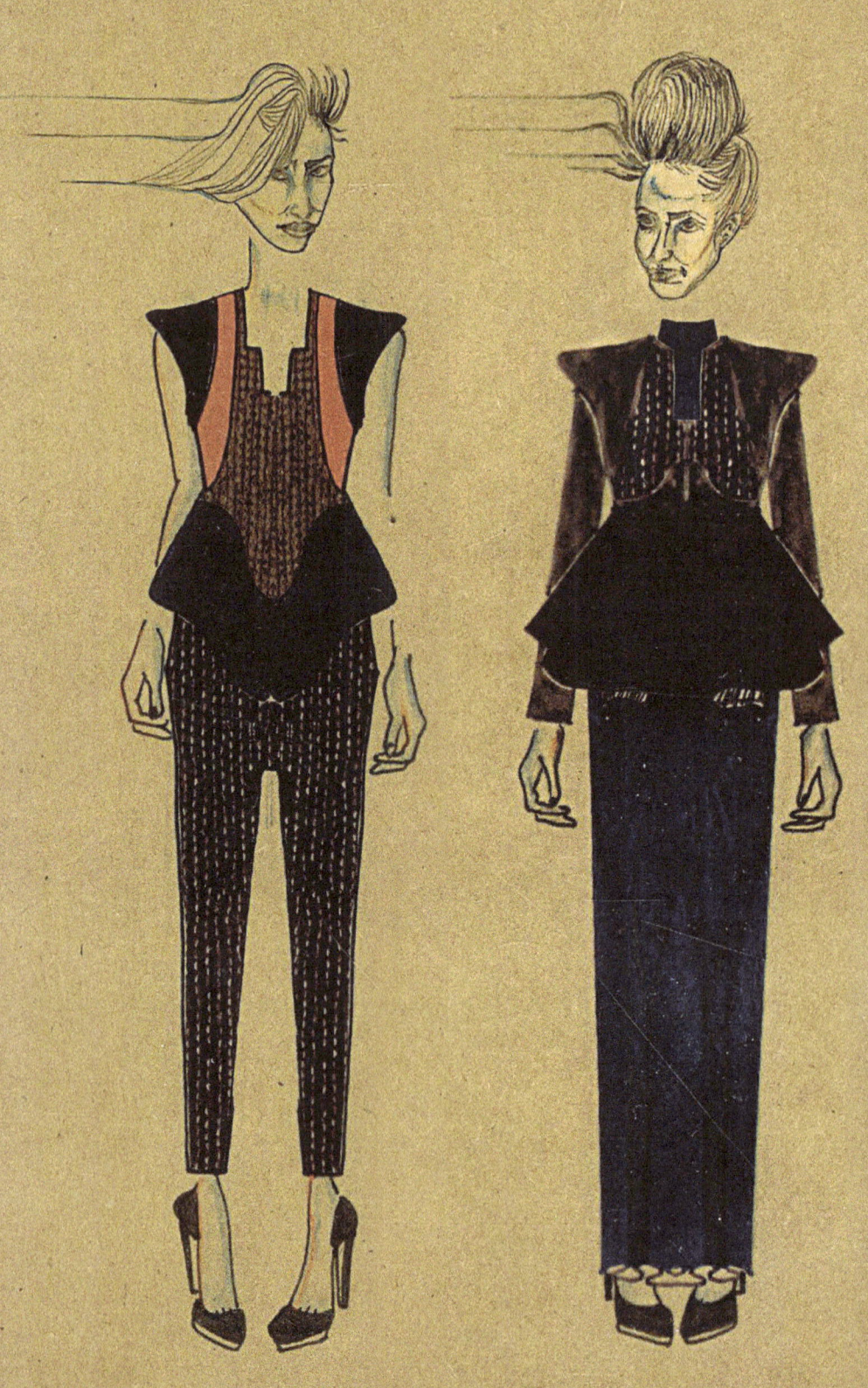

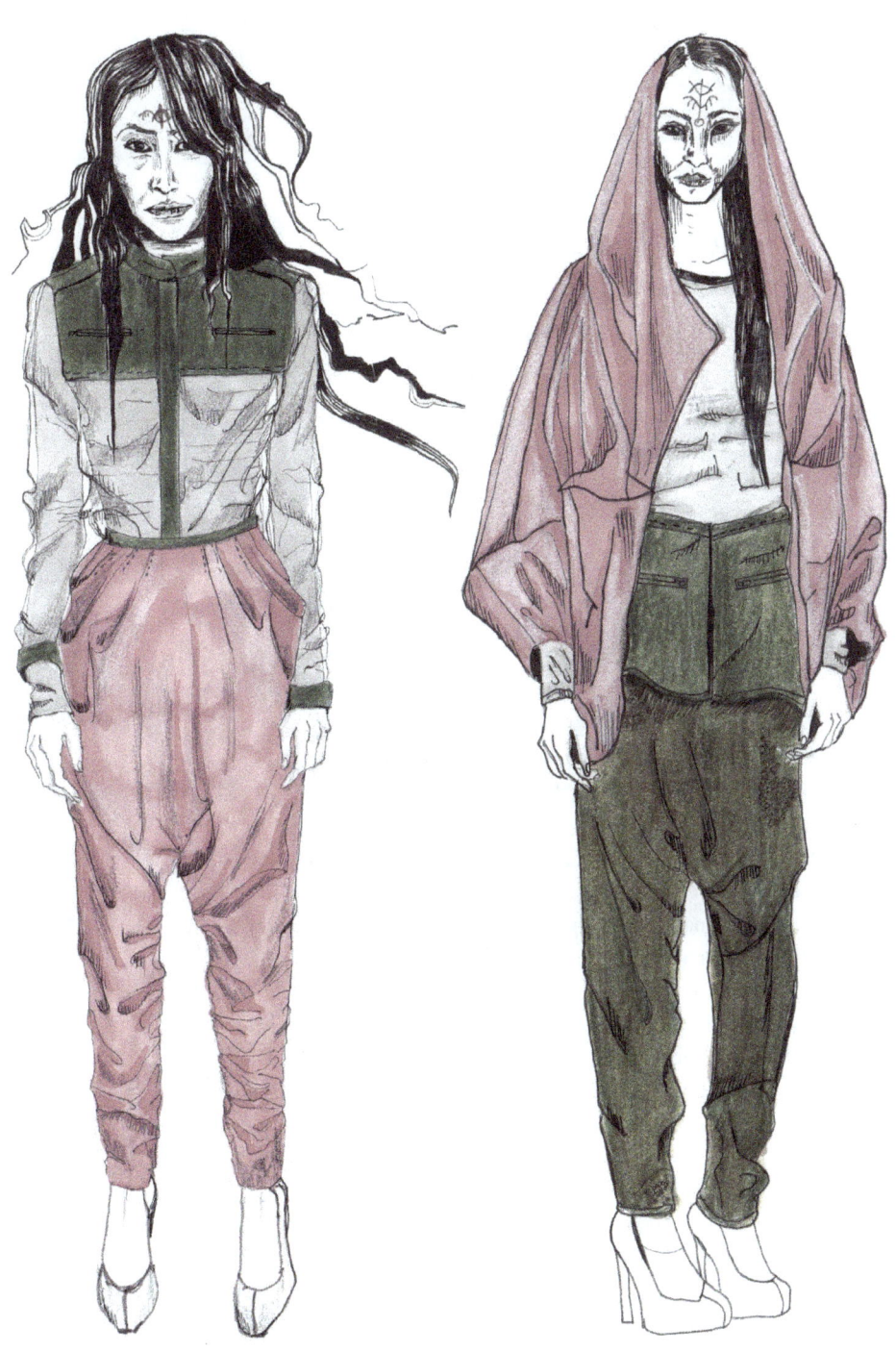

Opposite: *Untitled*, pen, coloured pencil collage of printed fabric textures on brown paper, 2009

This page: *Untitled*, pen and coloured pencil on paper, 2010

'Design helped me to discover
my passion for illustration
and made me not think too
much about my body image.'

Ese Akpojotor

SWEET DESIGN STUDIO

Ese Akpojotor is the UK-based illustrator and graphic
designer behind Sweet Design Studio. She began illustrating
after graduating in graphic design, and uses her work to
celebrate real life and the acceptance of who you are.
The silhouettes of Akpojotor's illustrations, both male
and female, are based on her own figure, a decision she
made to embrace her body in all its imperfections and
to share her personal story. She particularly draws on her
own teenage struggles to address issues of insecurity and
what society considers attractive or normal. Akpojotor's
illustrations are fun and colourful, characterized by simple
hand-drawn shapes, to which she adds paper-cut collages,
a technique she settled on after experimenting with many
others. Scanning and printing the collages as part of the
overall illustration results in a 3D effect, bringing volume
and texture to what would otherwise be a flat image.

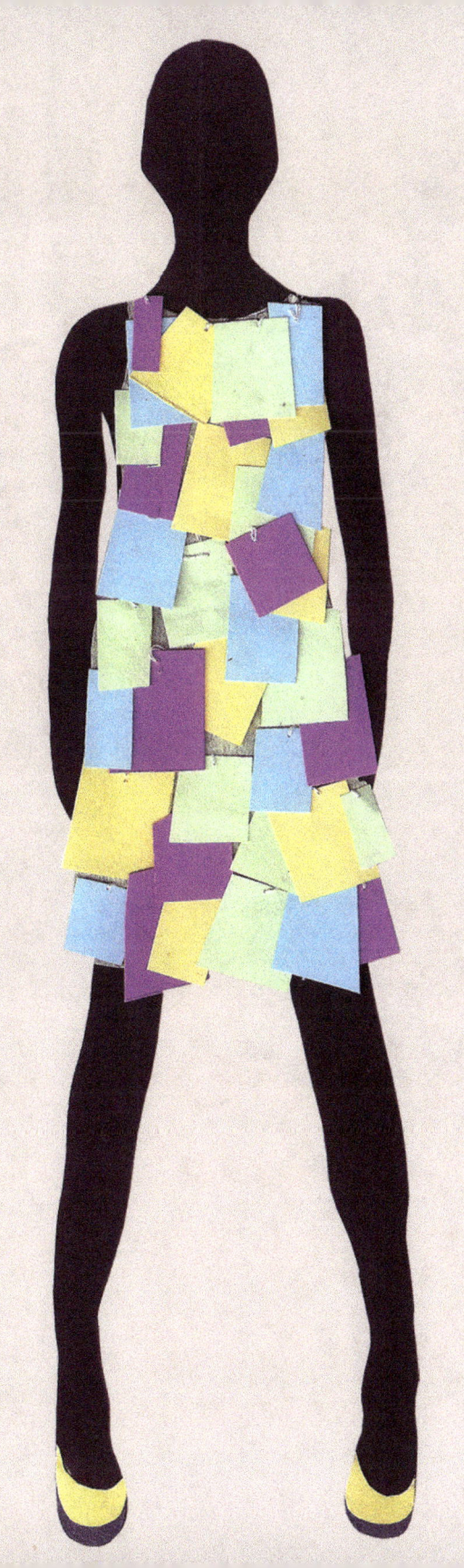

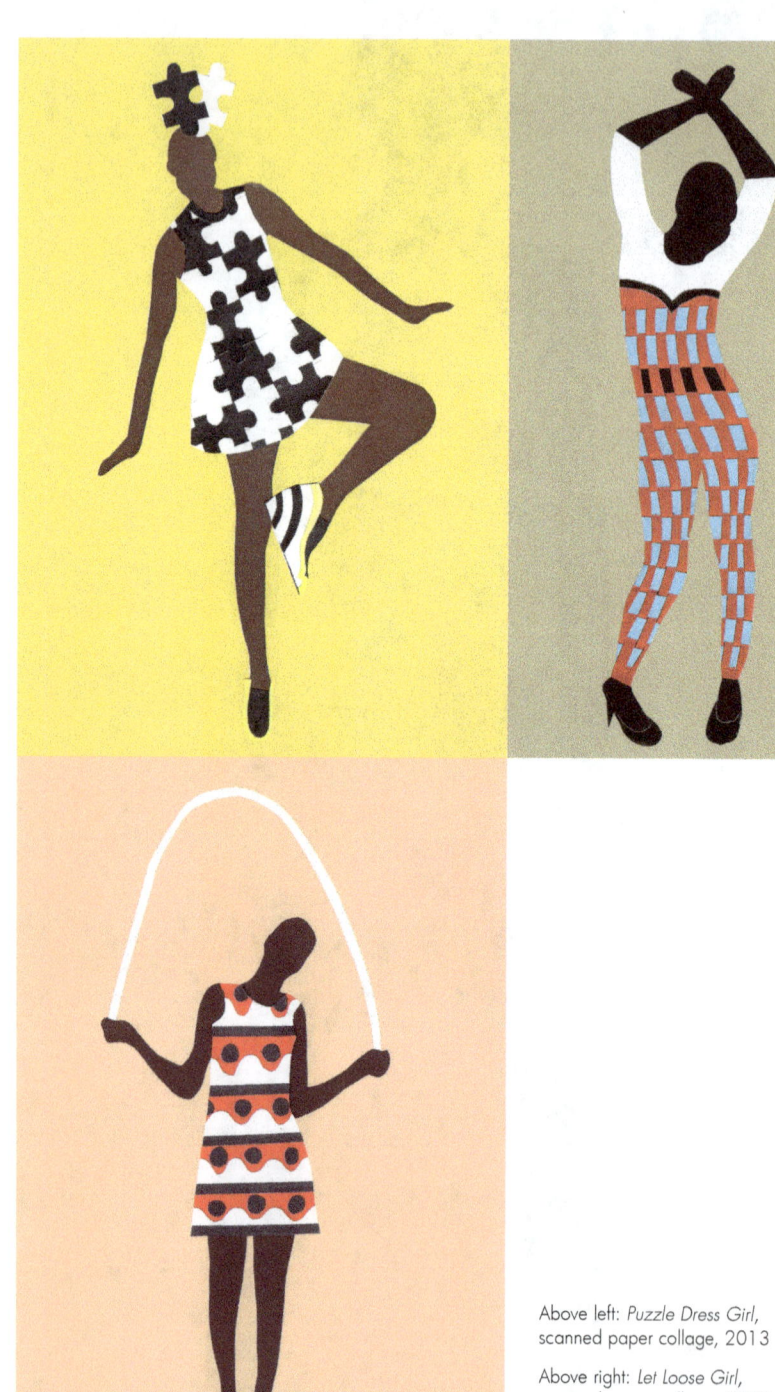

Above left: *Puzzle Dress Girl*,
scanned paper collage, 2013

Above right: *Let Loose Girl*,
scanned paper collage, 2009

Left: *Skipping Dress Girl*,
scanned paper collage, 2014

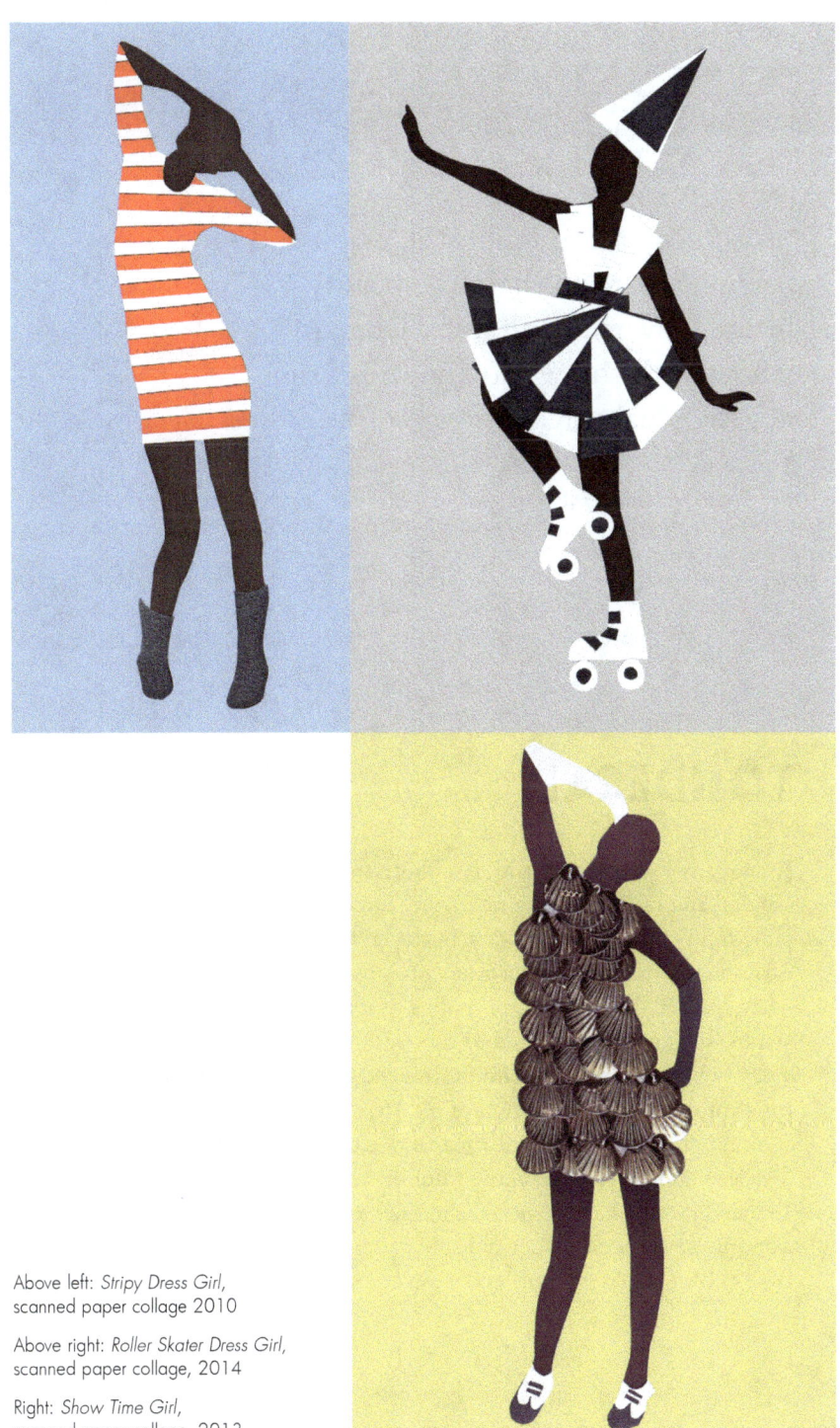

Above left: *Stripy Dress Girl*,
scanned paper collage 2010

Above right: *Roller Skater Dress Girl*,
scanned paper collage, 2014

Right: *Show Time Girl*,
scanned paper collage, 2013

'I want my art to empower, teach and inspire. I want to share the beauty, history, diversity and knowledge of Africa with the world and break the negative mainstream image of us.'

Tonderai

TONDERAI

Tonderai is a self-taught artist and illustrator. Born in South London and of Zimbabwean heritage, Tonderai's early influences came from comics and cartoons, but as he has grown older, African culture, music and artistic eras – namely Art Nouveau – have proven to be significant points of influence. He studied graphic design and attempted to carve out a career in the industry but, finding it unfulfilling, turned to art as a means of self-expression and exploration of his African heritage. Tonderai's fashion portraits of women form a large part of his portfolio, with depictions of style ranging from urban to traditional dress. Tonderai favours hand-drawn techniques over digital. Mainly working with pencil, he occasionally experiments with paint.

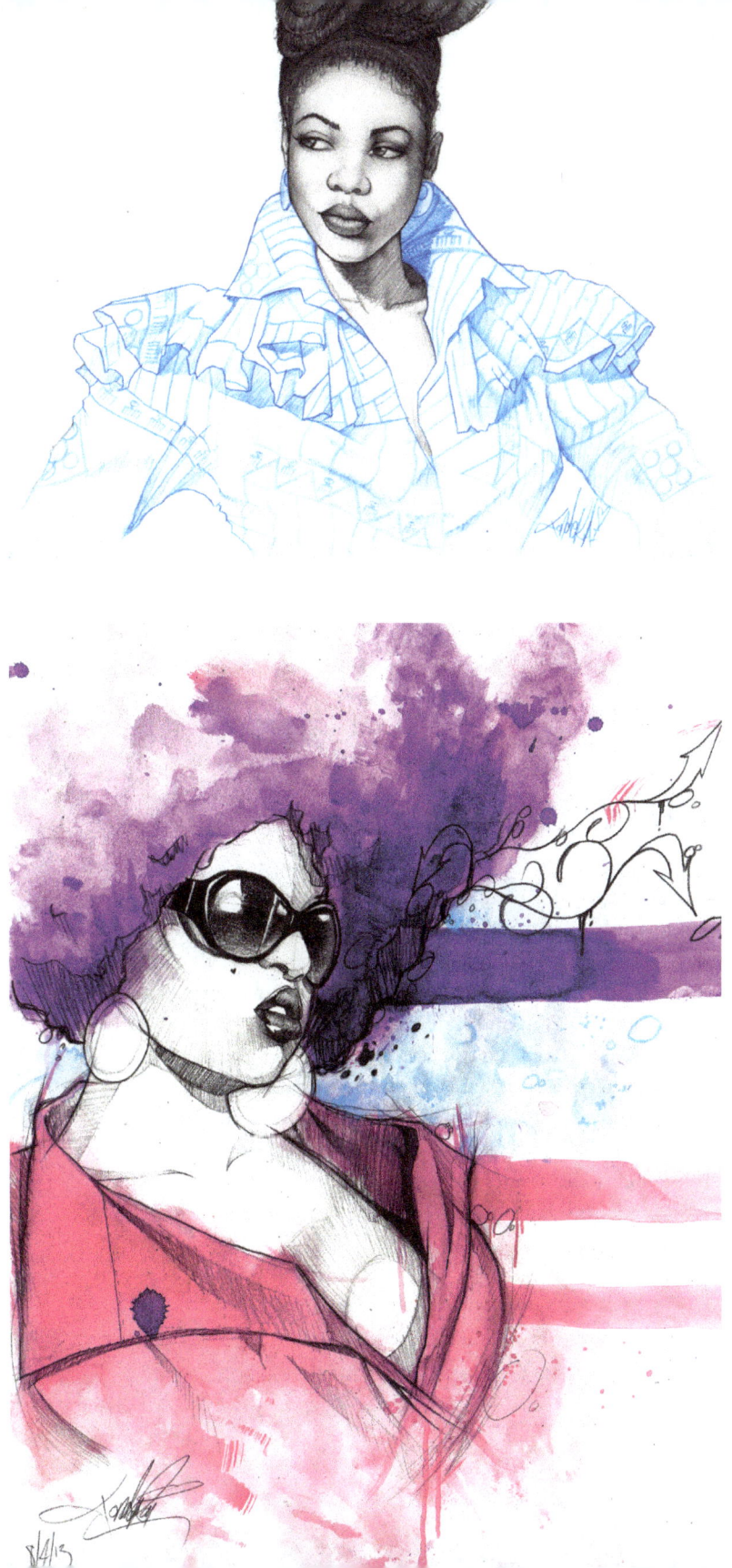

'Fashion illustration as my
focus point is greatly inspired by
everything contemporary African.
The nature and likewise the beauty,
the energy is really magical.'
UdegbunamTBJ

UDEGBUNAM TBJ

UdegbunamTBJ (Tochukwu Bernard Johnbosco) is a Nigerian
fashion illustrator whose illustrations are inspired by contemporary
Africa, in particular, drawing on the creative energy flowing through
the continent and the ever-popular African print fabrics. This
inspiration shows up in his illustrative style in the form of intricate,
free-flowing whorls and spirals, a defining characteristic of his
'Ankara Fabric Inspired' fashion illustration series. UdegbunamTBJ's
illustrations also fuse mixed-media, realism, Afro-futurism and
symbolism. He prefers drawing digitally, given the high degree
of flexibility that comes with the medium, but does not rule out
working with traditional mediums such as pencil and pen on paper.

Page 94: *Rebel Heart I*, digital illustration in Photoshop, 2015

Page 95 above left: *Untitled*, digital illustration in Photoshop, 2015

Page 95 above right: *Fro Muse1*, digital illustration in Photoshop, 2015

Page 95 below left: *Fro Muse2*, digital illustration in Photoshop, 2015

Page 95 below right: *Hipster*, digital illustration in Photoshop, 2015

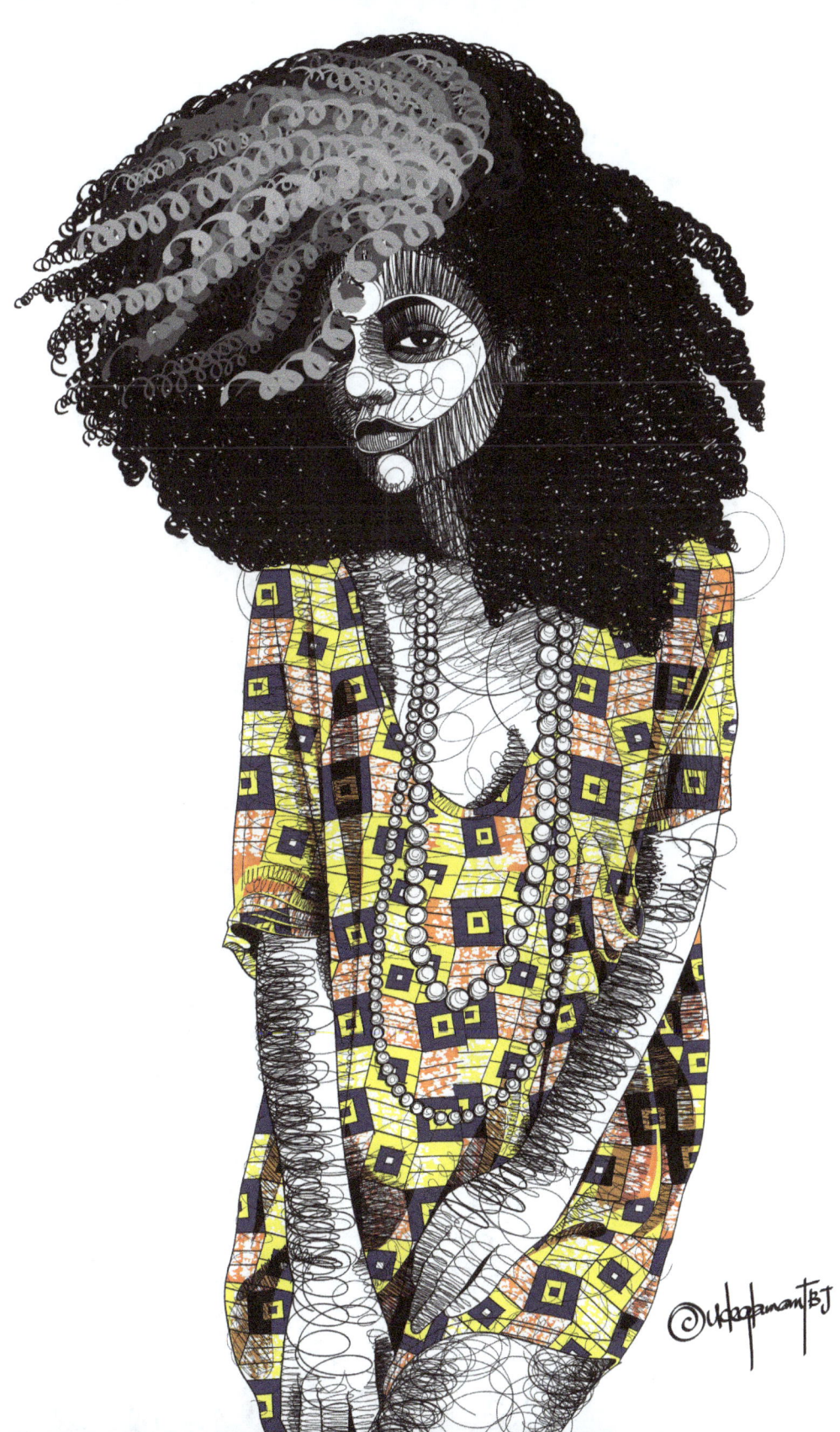

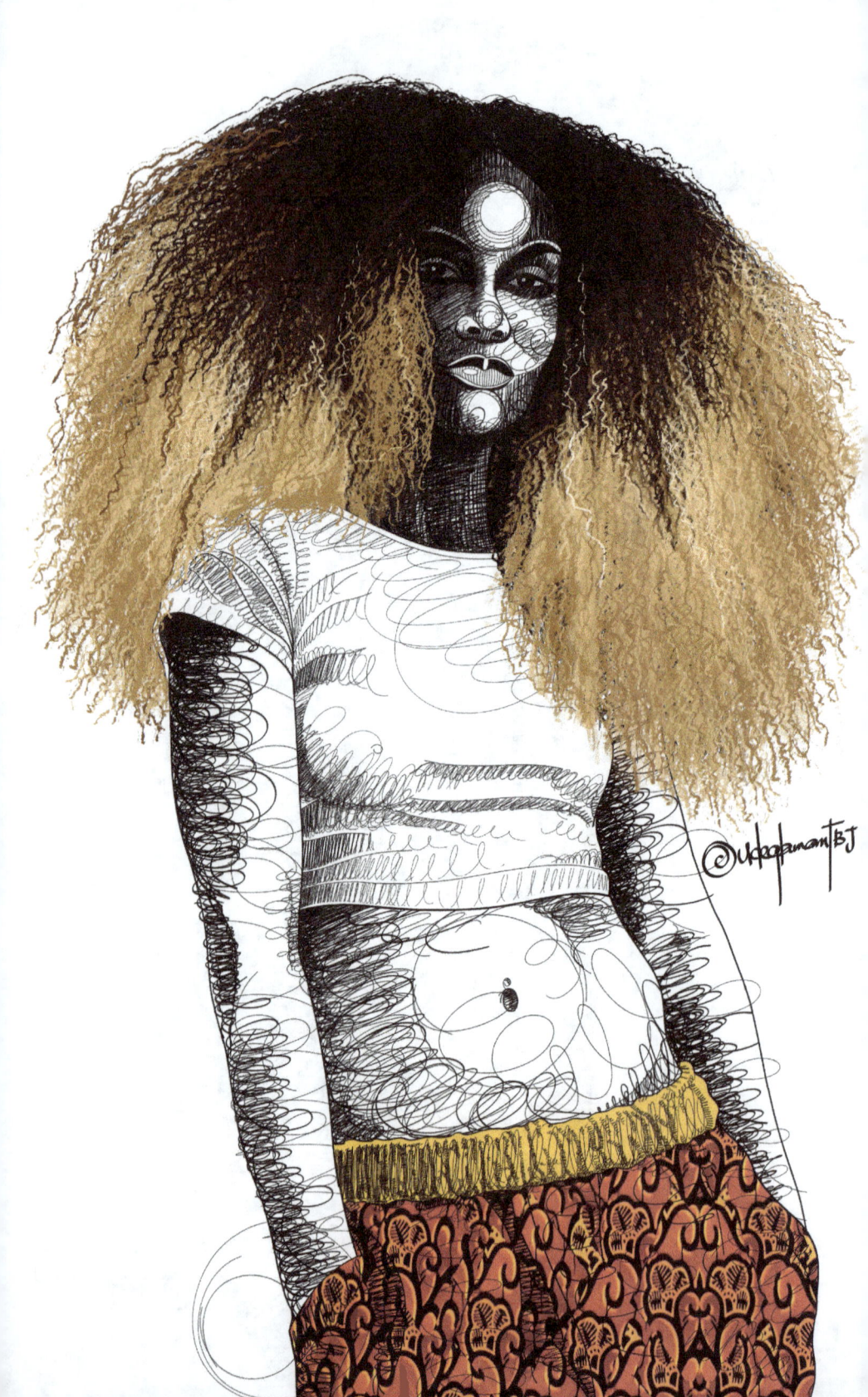

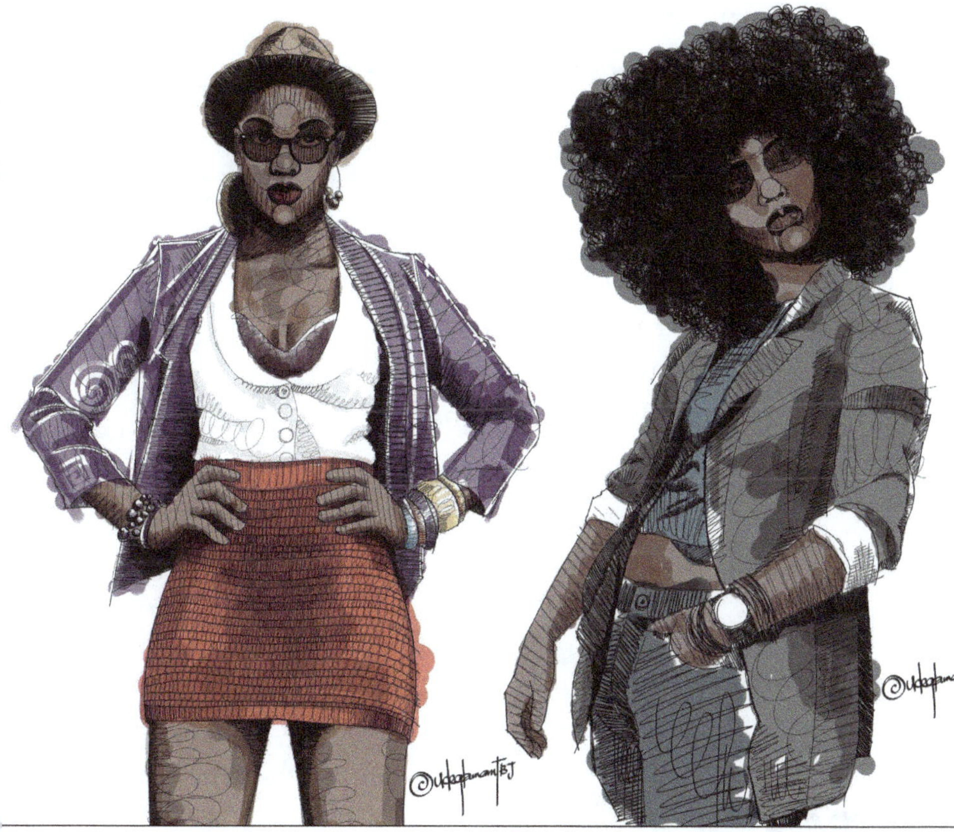

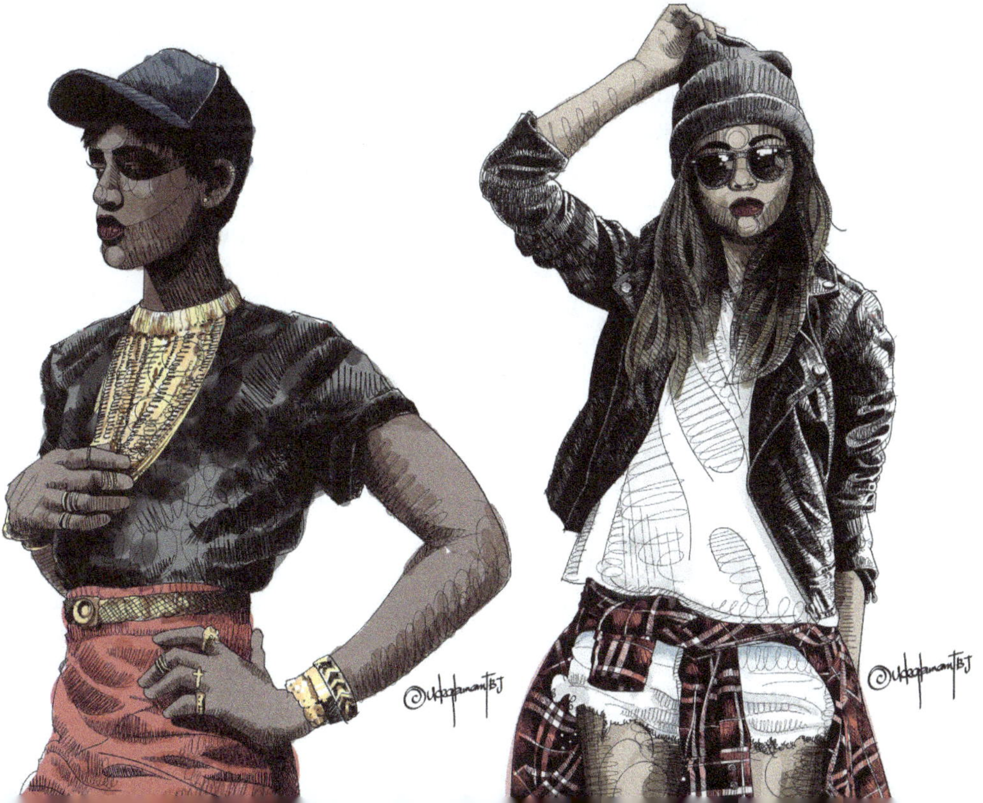

Opposite: *Coy*, watercolour, marker pen, ink and coloured pencil on paper, 2015

Page 98: *Turban Gang*, watercolour, marker pen, ink and coloured pencil on paper, 2015

Page 99: *Berry*, watercolour, marker pen, ink and coloured pencil on paper, 2015

'I am in love with basic pencil and ink ... hand-drawn art has a human essence to it that makes it more personal like handwriting.'

Yega

YEGA

Yega is a UK-based fashion illustrator. Her interest in the discipline began in her childhood, when she recalls spending her days creating little pageant line-ups, doodling, and sketching in her schoolbooks. African art, vivid colour schemes and pretty things inspire her. There is a refreshing femininity about Yega's illustrations. Her illustrative style is true to form and lifelike, characterized by the simplicity of black ink on white paper enhanced with the sheerness of watercolour. Like a number of her peers, Yega prefers hand-drawn techniques and predominately works with marker pen, ink, watercolour and pencil. She occasionally works with digital, citing her appreciation for the benefits that come with the ability to clean up and tweak her images if needed.

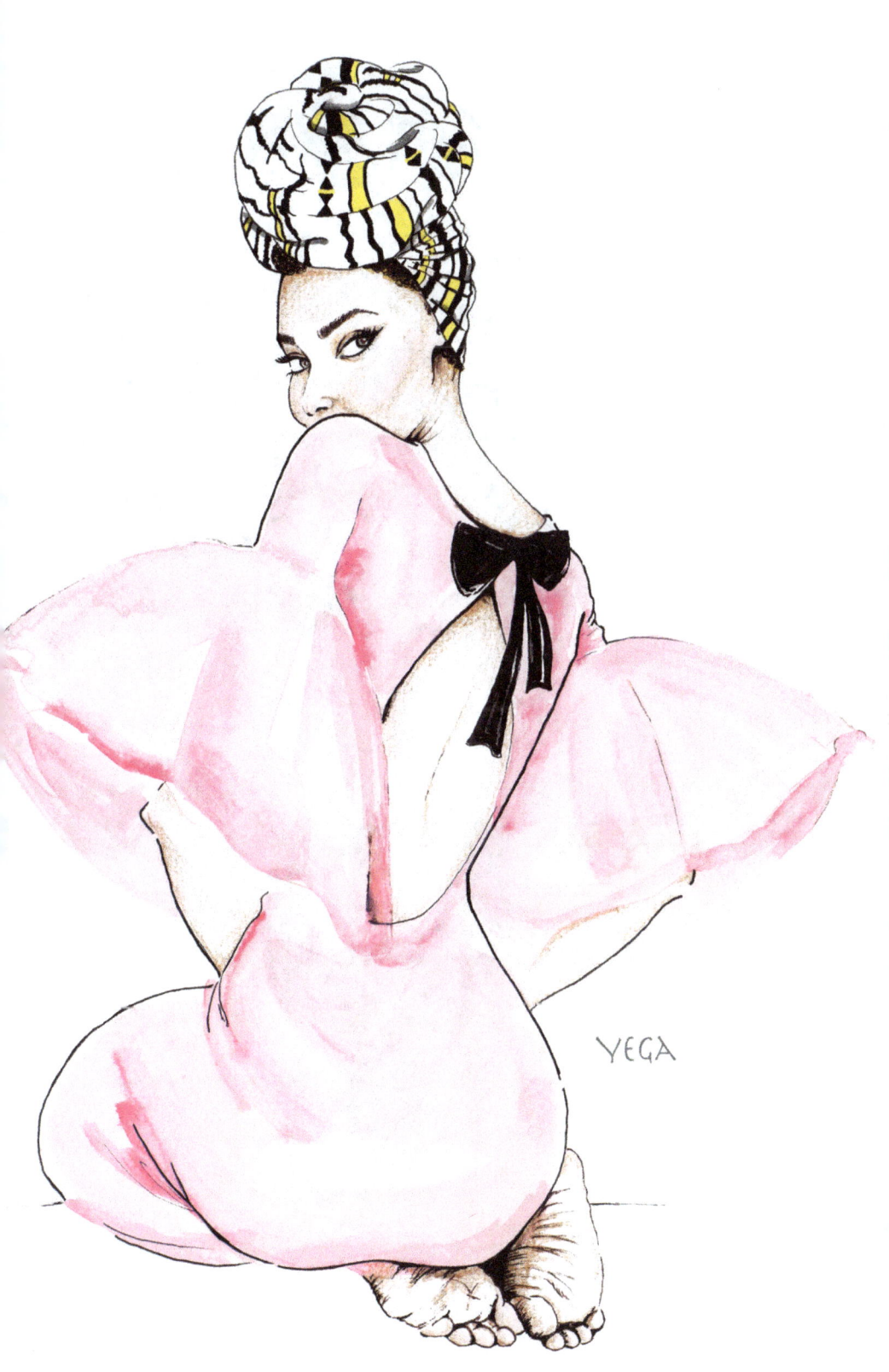

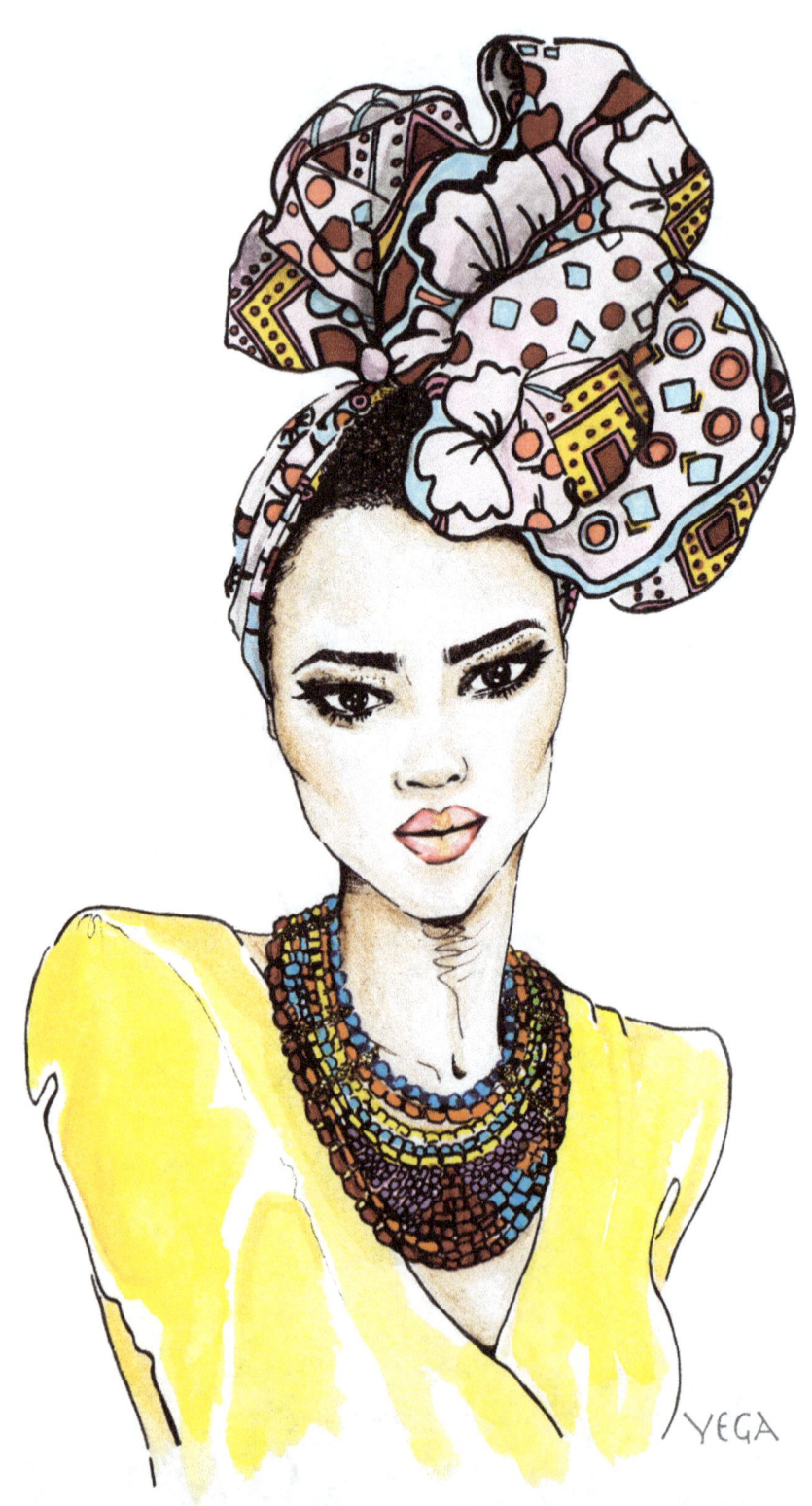

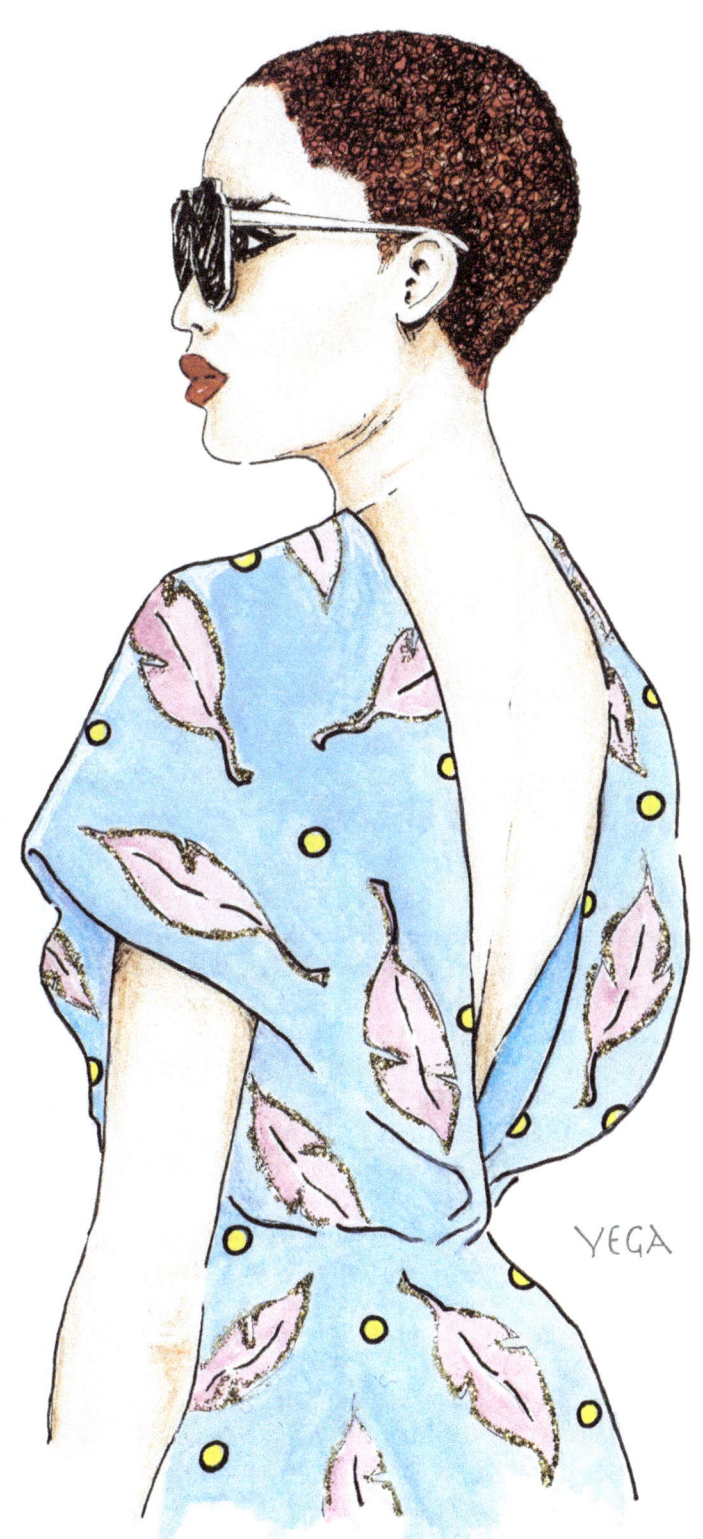

YEGA

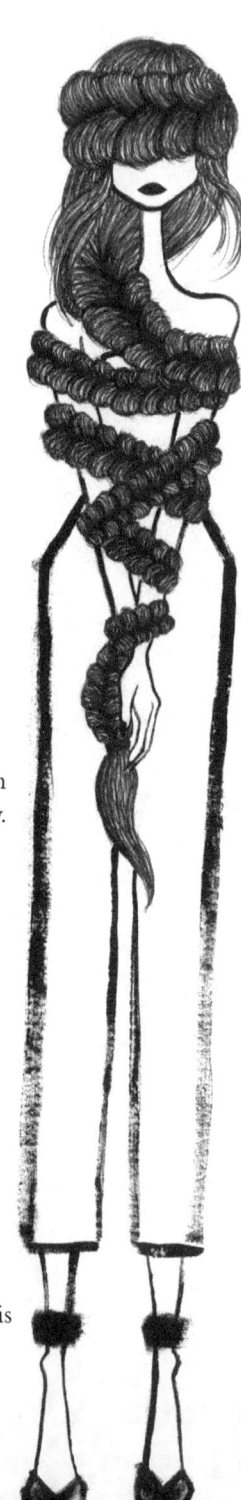

'... when expressing my taste in clothing was not possible because I could not find what I was looking for ... I would use fashion illustration as a way to design and document my sartorial viewpoints.'

Zakirah Rabaney

ZAKIRAH RABANEY

Zakirah Rabaney is a South African fashion illustrator, fashion editor, stylist and writer currently living in Munich, Germany. A career in fashion was inevitable for Rabaney, who cites taking style and fashion very seriously from a young age. Illustrating since she was eight years old, Rabaney has also been actively involved in South Africa's fashion industry as a fashion editor, stylist and trend analyst. Fashion illustration is Rabaney's way of exploring the relationship between form and fashion. She has always been influenced by her opinions about what kind of clothing and silhouettes suit the female form, and when seeking to communicate these opinions, would turn to illustration to design and document her ideas. Rabaney's illustrative style is expressive and bold. Working with pen or acrylic paint, she likes to use minimal lines in a dramatic way. And her preference for hand-drawn techniques serves to fully embrace the characteristics that an unsteady hand or unintended paint splatter adds to her illustrations. This she feels infuses some of 'an illustrator's personality onto the page, attesting to the originality and honesty of the work.'

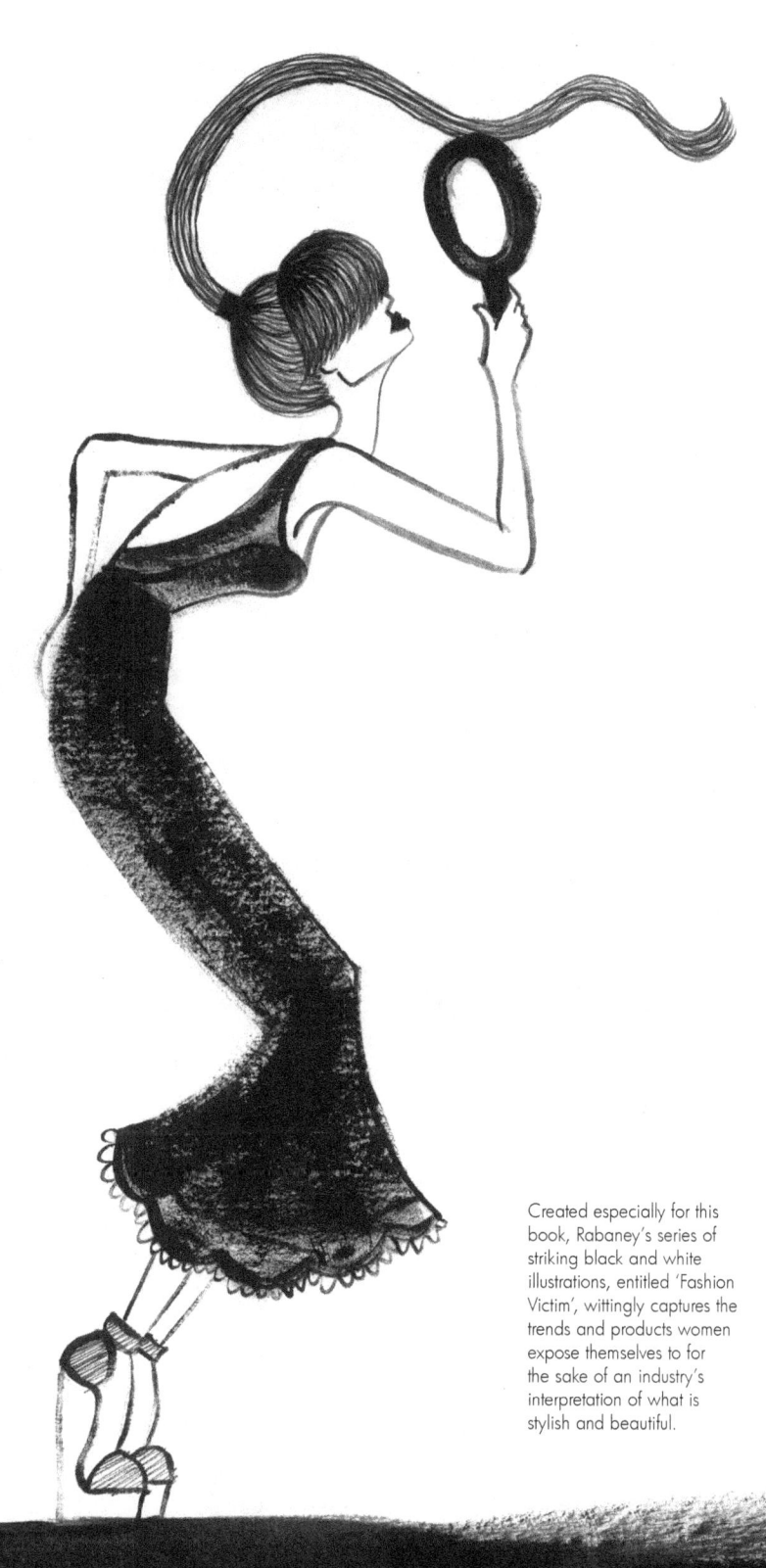

Created especially for this book, Rabaney's series of striking black and white illustrations, entitled 'Fashion Victim', wittingly captures the trends and products women expose themselves to for the sake of an industry's interpretation of what is stylish and beautiful.

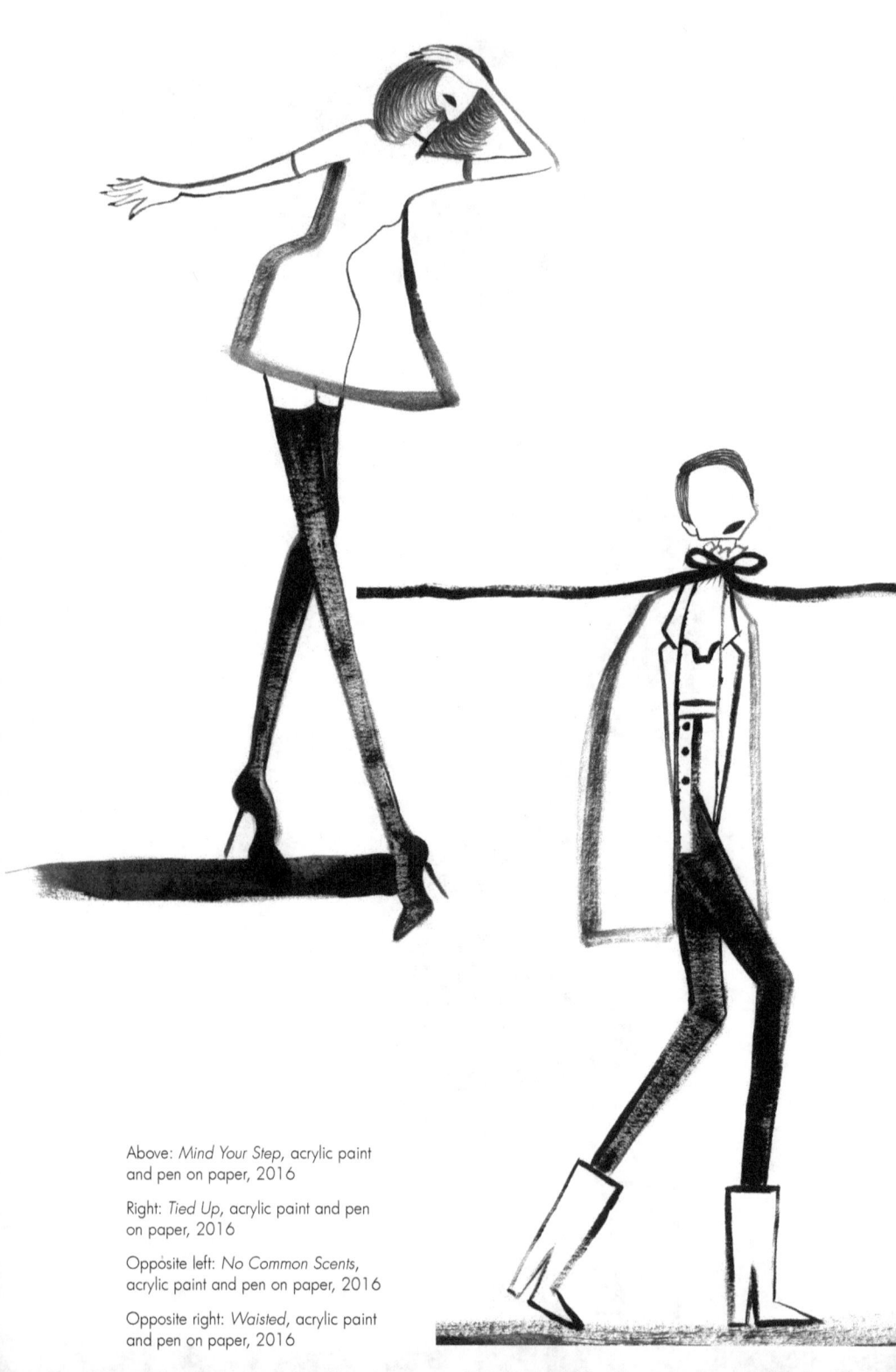

Above: *Mind Your Step*, acrylic paint and pen on paper, 2016

Right: *Tied Up*, acrylic paint and pen on paper, 2016

Opposite left: *No Common Scents*, acrylic paint and pen on paper, 2016

Opposite right: *Waisted*, acrylic paint and pen on paper, 2016

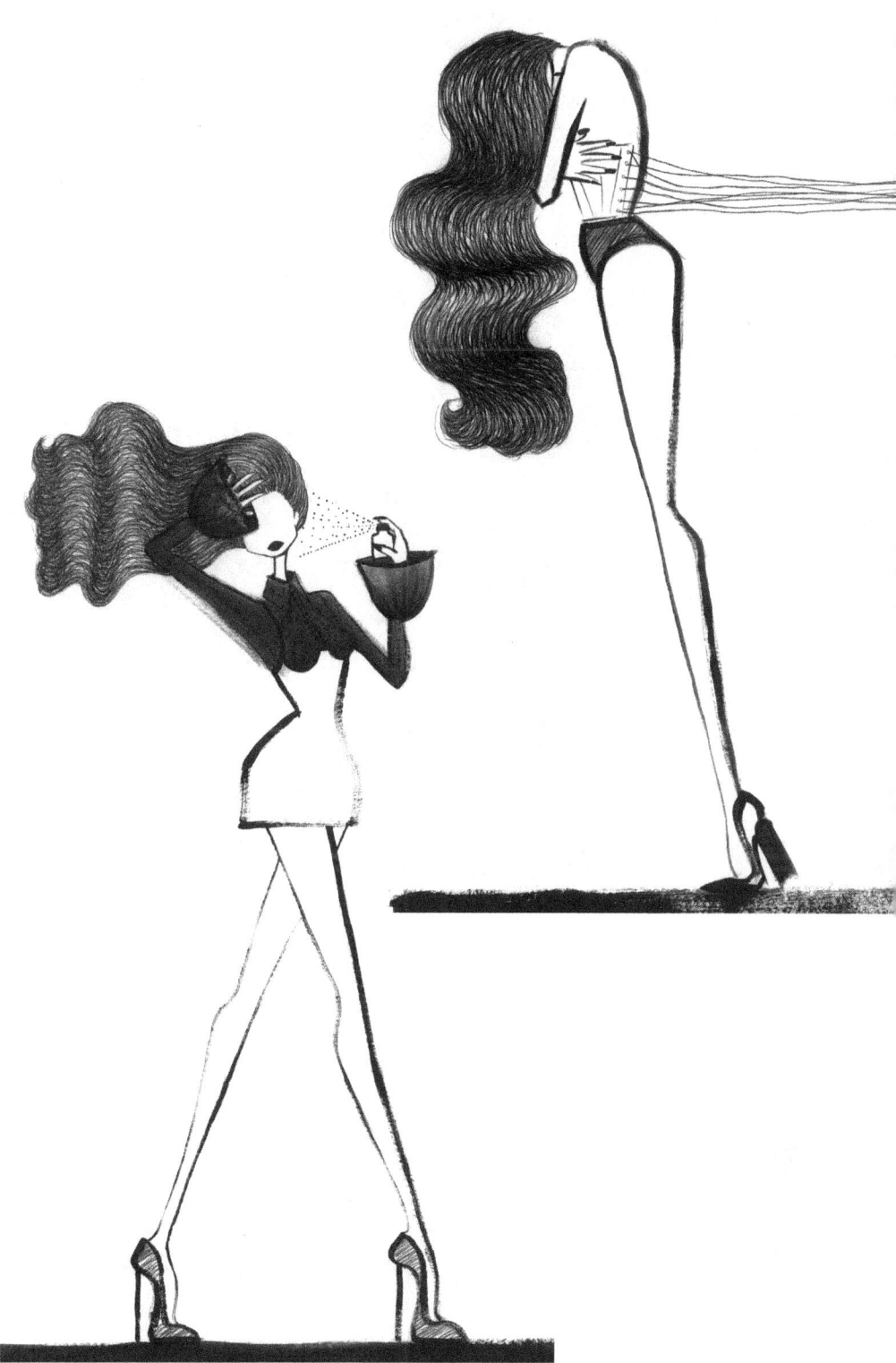

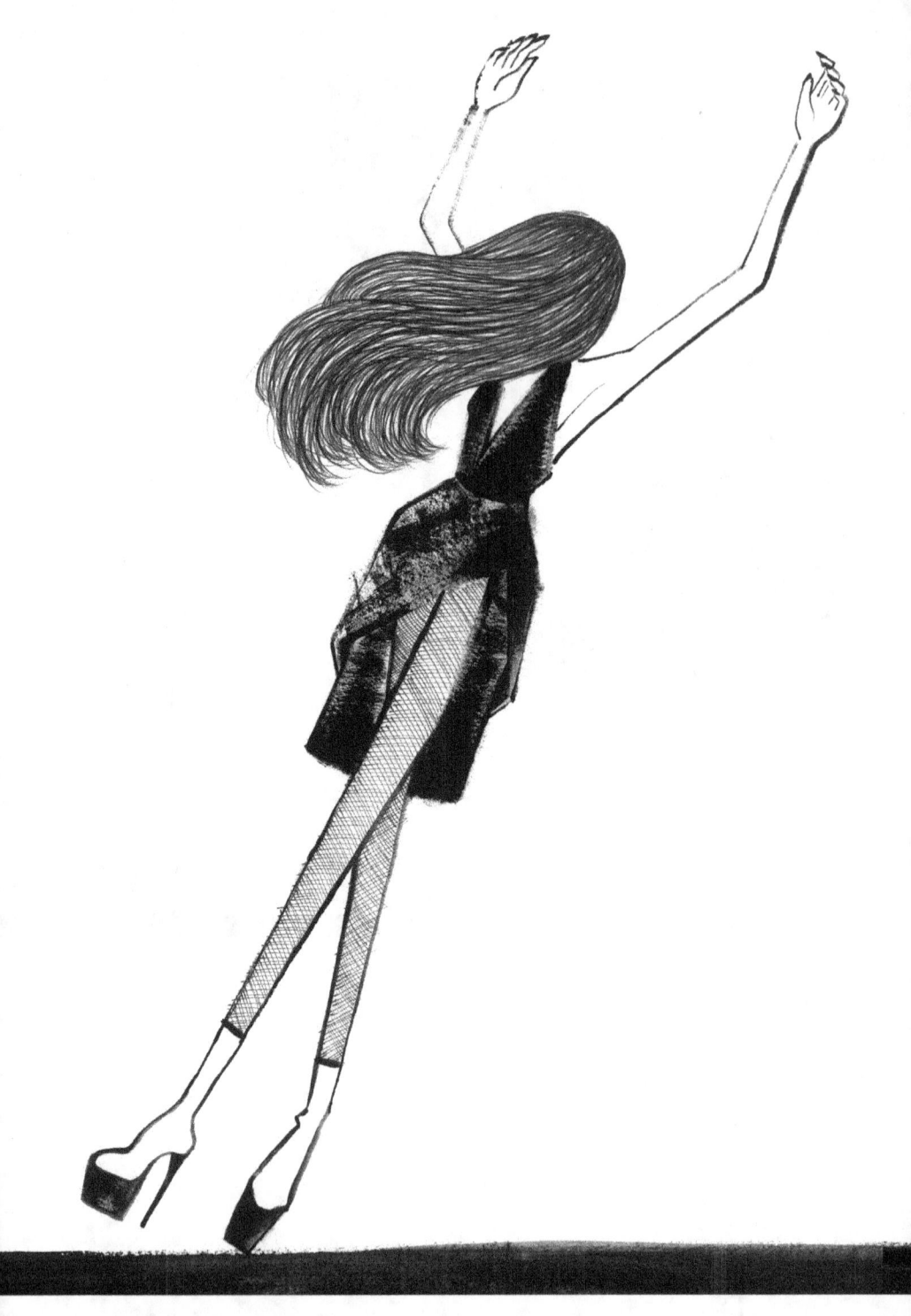

Flat-Fall Platform, acrylic paint and pen on paper, 2016

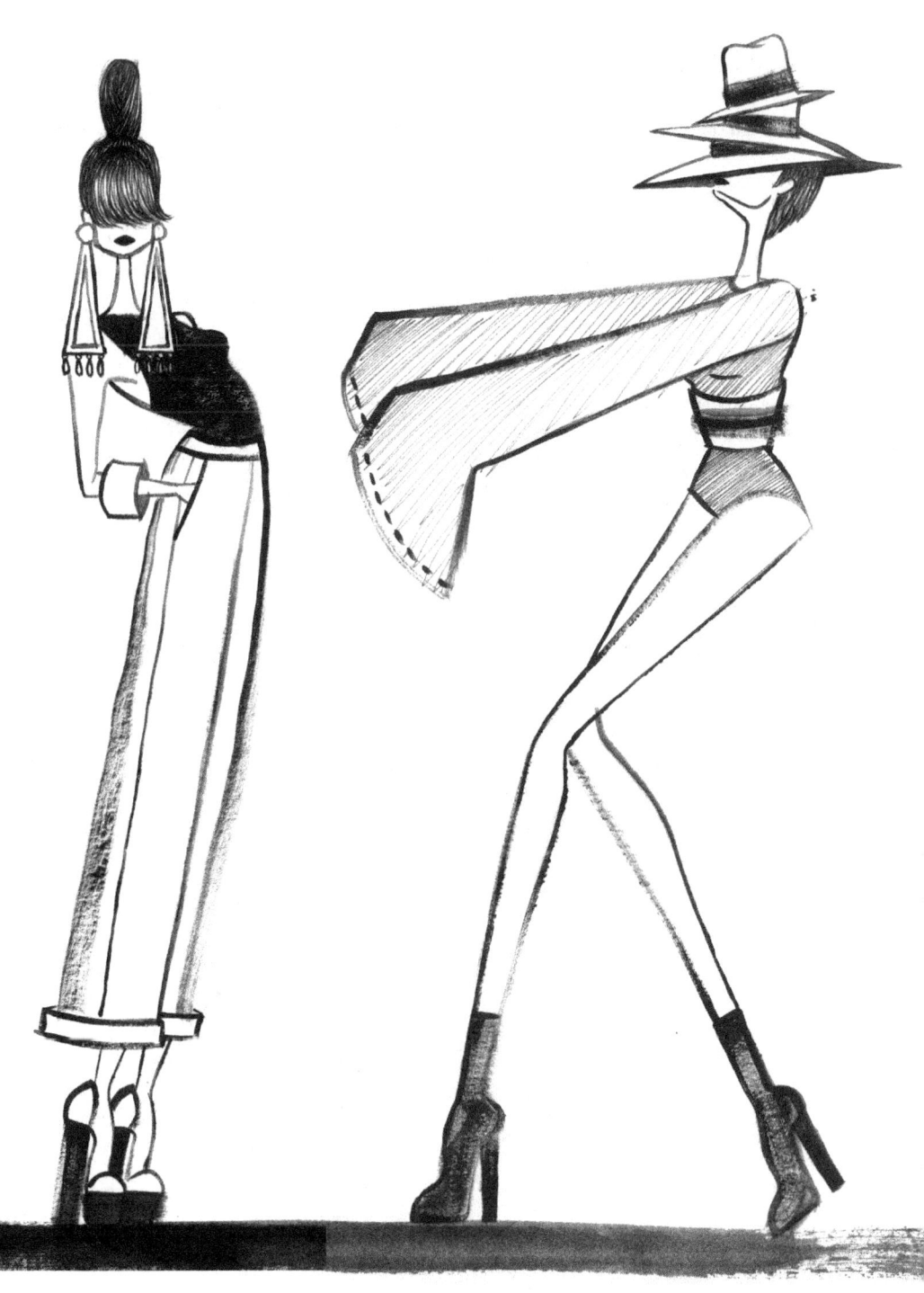

Left: *Dressed To Kill*, acrylic paint and pen on paper, 2016

Right: *Followers*, acrylic paint and pen on paper, 2016

CONTACTS

Adesola Lasisi
http://adesolalasisi.wixsite.com/illustrations

Claire Idera
http://www.claireidera.com

Ibe Ananaba
http://www.ibeananabart.com

Kobby Adu
http://www.kobeadu.wix.com/kaba

Kyere Kwaku Awiti
https://www.instagram.com/metakay

LeeAnn Visser
http://leeannvisser.wix.com/
fashionillustrations

Lindsay Dhludhlu
http://www.behance.net/lindsvydhludhlu

Michelle Njeri Cuthbert
http://www.theartofcarrying.com

Nanini
http://instagram.com/naninisart

Nathaniel Adjei Bio
http://www.instagram.com/y3fr3me_naethan

Nelly Aba Mensah
http://www.nellyaba.com

Nicole Cronje
http://www.nicolecronje.com

Nyorh Agwe
http://www.nyorhagwe.us

Okhai 'Lean Kid'
http://www.behance.net/okhai

Papa Oppong
http://www.instagram.com/papaoppong

Peniel Enchill
http://www.penielenchill.com

Pola Maneli
http://www.behance.net/polamaneli

Sonia Merabet
https://www.behance.net/sonish

Sweet Design Studio
http://www.sweetdesignstudio.co.uk

Tonderai
http://www.tonderaiarts.co.uk

UdegbunamTBJ
http://www.instagram.com/u_tbj

Yega
http://yegaillustrations.co.uk

Zakirah Rabaney
http://www.zakirahrabaney.com

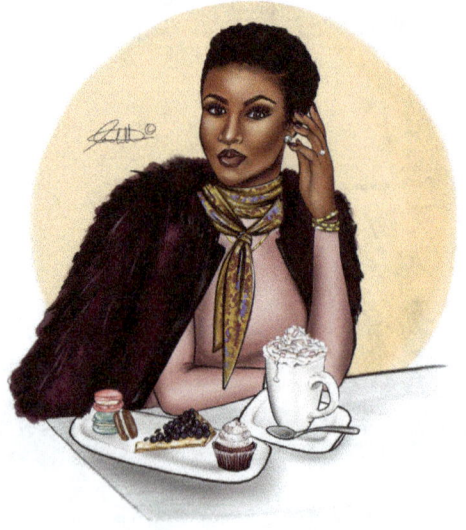

This page: Peniel Enchill, *November Beauty*,
digital illustration, 2015

Opposite: Nyorh Agwe, *MAASKS*, mixed media
(Photoshop, Illustrator, photographs of fabric
draping in cotton, silk, denim, wool, and canvas,
pen and marker pen on sketch paper), 2015

BIBLIOGRAPHY

Au Wai-man, R., 2004. 'The Future of Fashion Illustration'. [Online] Available at: http://ira.lib.polyu.edu.hk/handle/10397/3155 [Accessed 1 June 2016].

Battista , A., 2009. 'Early fashion publications'. [Online] Available at: http://irenebrination.typepad.com/irenebrination_notes_on_a/2009/07/early-fashion-publications.html [Accessed 11 April 2016].

Blackman, C., 2007. 100 Years of Fashion Illustration. London: Laurence King Publishing.

Blanco F., J., Doering, M. D., Hunt-Hurst, P. & Lee, H. V., 2015. Clothing and Fashion: American Fashion from Head to Toe. Santa Barbara: ANC-CLIO.

Hastie, P., 2013. 'Silk Road Secrets: The Buddhist Art of the Mogao Caves'. [Online] Available at: http://www.bbc.co.uk/arts/0/24624407 [Accessed 30 April 2016].

Europeana Fashion International Association, 2014. 'A Short History of Fashion Illustration'. [Online] Available at: http://blog.europeanafashion.eu/2014/06/12/history-fashion-illustration-europeana-fashio/ [Accessed 19 May 2016].

Jennings, H., 2011. New African Fashion. Munich: Prestel Publishing.

Kreis, S., 2011. 'Lecture 2: The Age of Discovery'. [Online] Available at: http://www.historyguide.org/earlymod/lecture2c.HTML [Accessed 19 May 2016].

McDowell, C., 2014. 'Colin's Column | Could Illustration Offer an Antidote to Fashion Banality?'. [Online] Available at: https://www.businessoffashion.com/articles/colins-column/colins-column-illustration-offer-antidote-fashion-banality [Accessed 28 May 2016].

Nevinson, J. L., 1967. Origin and Early History of the Fashion Plate. Washington, D.C.: Smithsonian Press.

Oppong, P., 2015. 'Creativity is a calling for Ghanaian designer'. [Online] Available at: http://edition.cnn.com/videos/world/2015/07/24/papa-oppong-african-voices-a.cnn [Accessed 24 August 2015].

Straus, D., 2014. 'Fashion, The High Life, and "The Duties of Married Females": 19th Century Fashion-Plate Magazines'. [Online] Available at: http://www.nypl.org/blog/2014/09/25/19th-century-fashion-plate-magazines [Accessed 10 June 2016].

Unwin, G., 2015. 'History of Publishing'. [Online] Available at: https://www.britannica.com/topic/publishing/Magazine-publishing [Accessed 12 June 2016].

IMAGE CREDITS

All the illustrations featured in this book are copyright © the individual illustrator, and shown according to their profile. Copyright © for: Front cover: UdegbunamTBJ; Back cover: Ibe Ananaba; Page 1: Papa Oppong; Page 2: Nathaniel Adjei Bio; Page 3: Okhai 'Lean Kid'; Page 4: Nanini; Page 5 Claire Idera; Page 7: Nelly Aba Mensah; Page 9: Okhai 'Lean Kid'; Page 13: Lindsay Dhludhlu; Page 14-15: Papa Oppong; Page 106: Peniel Enchill; Page 107: Nyorh Agwe; Page 108: Nelly Aba Mensah.

ACKNOWLEDGEMENTS

Tapiwa Matsinde: Bringing a book to life is a magical experience, one that draws on the talents of many. A huge thank you to all the illustrators who gave generously to share their work and make this book possible. My heartfelt thanks to Zakirah Rabaney for contributing the introduction, and being a sounding board. To Ellen Christie for helping us shape our manuscript. To all my family and friends whose support makes it possible to do what I love. To you, the reader holding this book in your hand, your support helps spread the word.

And, above all, in everything I do I give YOU thanks.

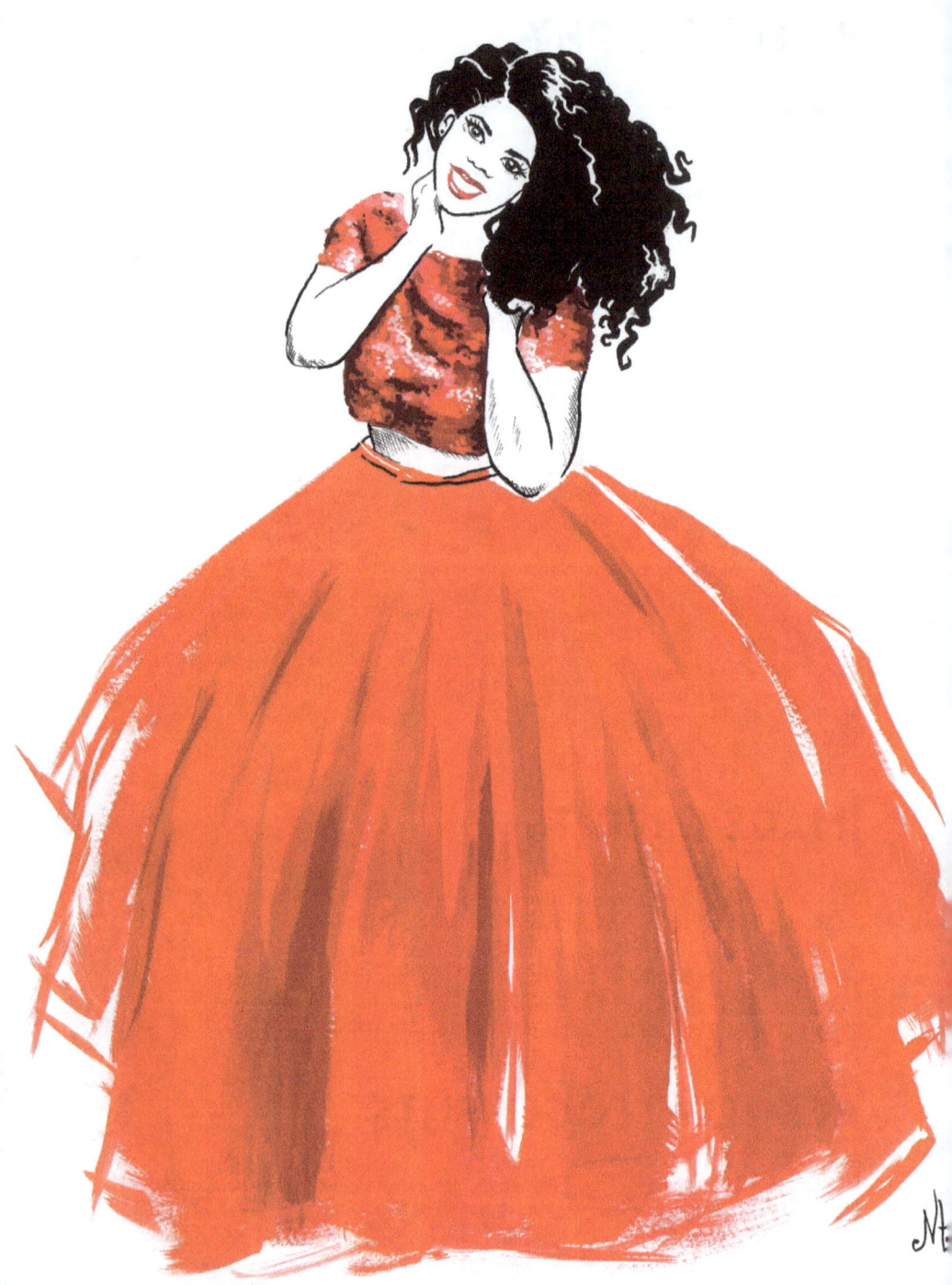

Nelly Aba Mensah, *Birthday Girl*, gouache and ink on paper, 2016

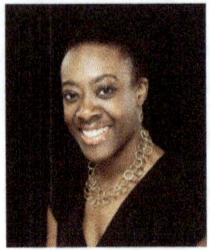

Photo credit: Tapiwa Matsinde

Tapiwa Matsinde is a British-born graphic designer, author, independent writer and blogger of Zimbabwean heritage. She writes about Africa's growing contemporary creative industries for her blog, *Atelier Fifty-Five*, and is the author of *Contemporary Design Africa*.

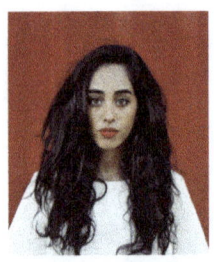

Photo credit: Niquita Bento

Zakirah Rabaney is a fashion editor, stylist and trend analyst who has worked in the South African fashion industry. Long before this, she was creating fashion illustrations. The blend of her intelligent perspective and creative talent crafts a discerning story about a new generation of African creatives, their artistic viewpoints on fashion, as well as the challenges that come with being an African fashion illustrator today.

www.ingramcontent.com/pod-product-compliance
Lightning Source LLC
Chambersburg PA
CBHW072149170526
45158CB00004BA/1570